Frommer's®

24 GREAT walks in ROME

2nd Edition

WILEY

Wiley Publishing, Inc.

Author: Jennifer Griffiths
Commissioning Editor: Donna Wood
Art Editor: Alison Fenton
Page layout: Andrew Milne
Proofreader: Polly Boyd
Picture Researcher: Alice Earle
Cartography provided by the Mapping Services
Department of AA Publishing
Production: Stephanie Allen

Edited, designed and produced by AA Publishing.
© AA Media Limited 2008. Reprinted January 2010
This edition revised and updated June 2010

Published by AA Publishing.

Published in the United States by
Wiley Publishing, Inc.
111 River Street, Hoboken, NJ 07030

Find us online at Frommers.com

Frommer's is a registered trademark of Arthur Frommer.
Used under license.

Mapping in this title produced from:
Map data © MAIRDUMONT/Falk Verlag 2010
All rights reserved

ISBN 978-0-470-92816-5

A04510

A CIP catalogue record for this book is available from the
British Library.

Printed in China by Leo Paper Group

OPPOSITE: TREVI FOUNTAIN

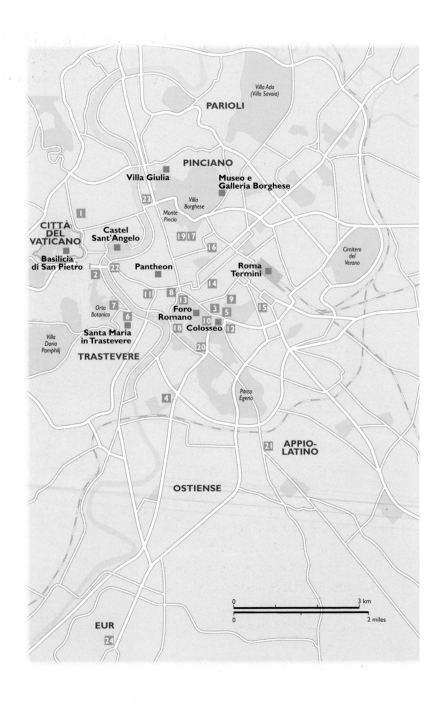

PARIOLI

Villa Àda (Villa Savoia)

PINCIANO

Villa Giulia

Museo e Galleria Borghese

23

Villa Borghese

1

Monte Pincio

CITTÀ DEL VATICANO

Castel Sant'Angelo

19 17

16

Basilicia di San Pietro

2 22

Pantheon

Roma Termini

Cimitero del Verano

11 8

14

Foro Romano

13

9

3 5

15

7

Orto Botanico

6

10

18 **Colosseo**

12

Villa Doria Pamphilj

Santa Maria in Trastevere

20

TRASTEVERE

4

Parco Egerio

APPIO-LATINO

21

OSTIENSE

0   3 km

0   2 miles

EUR

24

CONTENTS

Introduction

The Roman poet Rutilius Namatianus once wrote of his city: 'To count up the glories of Rome is like counting the stars in the sky', and it is true to say that Rome's countless glories, as well as its endless history and mystery, are what make Rome the indisputably Eternal City.

Rome is an icon of human history – a place where the most passionate intrigues of love, war and power have been played out for nearly 3,000 years. It is a city where you can enjoy extraordinary museums, fine dining and a relaxed atmosphere against a backdrop that has witnessed the course of Western civilization.

Rome is a unique metropolis, where ancient and modern exist side by side. When you start to explore the city, it helps to have some knowledge of the transport system. There are just two underground lines fully in operation at the moment, with two more lines currently under construction. Archaeologists and engineers are working closely together to plough through the buried layers of the ancient city and, unsurprisingly, progress is slow. The city's three tramlines do not serve the centre; the bus system is the best way to get from A to B, but it is infamously unreliable. Yellow signs mark the bus stops or *fermate*. Under each bus number is the list of stops on the route. A red box appears around the stop you are standing at.

Metro, bus and tram tickets, *biglietti*, are one and the same. You can buy them from any station ticket office, *biglietteria*, or from most bars. Public transport passes are available for those visiting for longer. Taxis in Rome don't generally stop if you try to wave them down, but you can pick one up at any stand marked by an orange TAXI sign. Fortunately, Rome is built on a human scale and, if you choose to, you can walk nearly everywhere.

Opening times can be the source of some confusion. Museums are closed on Mondays (with the exception of the Vatican Museums, which do not operate under the rules of the Italian government). Most shops outside the centre are closed in the afternoons between 1.30 and 4.30pm. After a welcome siesta, they reopen until 8pm. Most small churches have a similar timetable. You will often find them open in the mornings before noon and then again after 4pm. Keep these times in mind when you are touring the city.

The walks in this book are designed to help you explore some of the countless glories of Rome, from the unparalleled richness of the Vatican's art collections (Walk 1), to the austere Fascist architecture of the EUR district (Walk 24). You will enjoy some of the less crowded parts of the city on these walks. Take time to wander aimlessly through the backstreets and alleys, for they often reveal the true character of the city. The once right-angled and straight streets of ancient Rome were mostly replaced by the baffling and winding alleyways of medieval times, but don't be afraid of getting lost in hidden corners of the city. That's all part of your romantic Roman adventure.

Virtue and Vice in Vatican City

The labyrinthine Vatican Museums contain some of the world's richest art. Over four million people a year view the ceiling in the Sistine Chapel.

Vatican City is the smallest city-state in the world. It has been the residence of the popes since the 14th century, when they returned to Rome from Avignon after a 70-year absence. On their return, the popes used art and architecture to reassert their spiritual and temporal authority over the city. This period of unequalled artistic patronage fed the development of the Renaissance and Baroque, and artists flocked to Rome. The popes were, in effect, kings of Rome until 1870. When the creators of the new Italian nation conquered Rome, Pope Pius IX went into voluntary exile inside the Vatican. He died in 1877, having never left the palace again. The division between the church and the new state continued until the 1929 Lateran Pact, when Mussolini was hungry for political power and, in exchange for much-needed political support from the Holy See, allowed the creation of this independent theocracy within Rome. Over the past five centuries the Vatican palace has grown into a complex of long corridors connecting some 11,500 rooms. Expect long queues from May to September.

Take Metro Line A to Ottaviano. Follow signs to San Pietro, heading south from the metro on Via Ottaviano to Piazza del Risorgimento. Turn right and follow the walls round Viale Bastioni di Michelangelo, turning left up Viale Vaticano to the museum entrance.

On the south side of the square you will see a corner of the Vatican City walls. The Leonine walls, as they are known, were built by Pope Leo IV in the 9th century after Saracens from North Africa sailed up the Tiber in 846 and raided the riches of St Peter's basilica. Michelangelo helped to re-fortify the walls around the Vatican, and this stretch is named after him. Expect to queue alongside these walls. **VATICAN CITY;** CLOSED SUN. CHECK OPENING HOURS BEFORE VISITING. www.vatican.va

2 Enter the museums through the modern entrance doors and proceed through the security checks.

This is the only public entrance to Vatican City. After passing security you can hire a museum guide or book a tour of the gardens, which are restricted to guided tours only. In the ancient world this area was called Vatican Hill, and not much has changed – you can see the hill rising above the walls before you enter. Before the 4th century this spot was the site of a large pagan necropolis.

3 Head upstairs to buy tickets, and take the escalator to the entrance landing. Before you is a breathtaking

WHERE TO EAT

🍴 OLD BRIDGE GELATERIA, Viale dei Bastioni di Michelangelo 5; Tel: 06 39723026. Tiny *gelateria* with great ice cream; generous servings, central location.

🍴 DA BENITO E GILBERTO AL FALCO, Via del Falco 19; Tel: 06 6867769. Always packed. Famous for seafood. 🍴 L'ISOLA DELLA PIZZA, Via degli Scipioni 47; Tel: 06 39733483. Near the metro; serves good pizza.

view of St Peter's dome. Turn right on the landing and then turn immediately left for the Pinacoteca or painting gallery.

These galleries are home to Giotto's *Stefaneschi Triptych* (c.1313), thought to have been painted for Old St Peter's. You will also find the last work ever painted by Raphael before he died at 37, probably from a venereal disease. *The Transfiguration* (1520) was carried in his funeral procession along with his body. Make sure you see the only Leonardo painting in Rome, *St Jerome in the Wilderness* (c.1480). Even in its damaged and unfinished state, the painting reveals Leonardo's mastery of human anatomy. And don't miss Caravaggio's dramatic *Deposition,* in which it seems as if Christ's body is being passed to you.

OPPOSITE: GOLDEN SPHERE OUTSIDE THE VATICAN MUSEUMS

DISTANCE 1 mile (1.6km)

ALLOW 3 hours

START Ottaviano San Pietro Metro

FINISH Ottaviano San Pietro Metro or bus from Via della Conciliazione

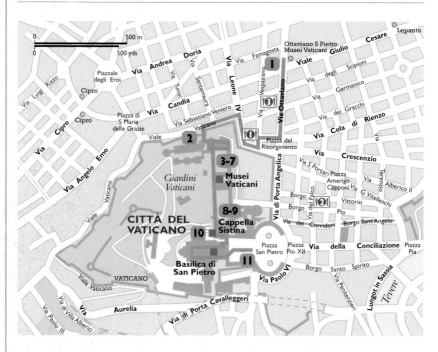

4 Leave the Pinacoteca and return to the entrance landing. Turn left this time, to the courtyard of the Pinecone.

This rectangular courtyard holds a bronze pinecone that once decorated a fountain in the courtyard of Old St Peter's. When the new St Peter's was built in 1506, the old church was demolished, but the pinecone miraculously survived. Legend has it that the pinecone has a pagan past, and originally decorated the end of a staff that was part of a statue of Bacchus.

5 Walk straight through the courtyard. Climb the stairs to your left. You are now entering the ancient galleries. Turn left and walk into the Belvedere courtyard.

This famous courtyard takes its name from the view from the landing; *bel* means beautiful and *vedere*, view. Donato Bramante built it for Pope Julius II to house his ever-expanding collections of ancient statuary, which once formed the basis of the Vatican Museums. In the four

niches you can admire: *Apollo Belvedere*, praised as the supreme achievement of classical Greek sculpture; Antonio Canova's *Perseus* (1797-1801), purchased by the Vatican after Napoleon plundered Rome; a 1st-century BC Roman copy of *Hermes* after Praxiteles; and the famous Laocoön group, described by Pliny, which was rediscovered in 1506. The farmer who found the statue received a lifetime stipend from the pope. It depicts the Trojan priest who warned against Greeks bearing gifts – the original right arm of the statue was found four centuries later.

6 Proceed through the Room of Animals, filled with animal sculpture and a floor from a Roman aviary, into the Room of the Muses, Room of the Rotunda and Room of the Greek Cross.

The *Belvedere Torso* stands at the centre of the Room of the Muses. Michelangelo

admired it greatly and used it as a model for Christ in *The Last Judgment* of the Sistine Chapel. The Room of the Rotunda is named and modelled after the Pantheon and houses a fountain basin made from a single piece of rare porphyry marble. In the Room of the Greek Cross you will see the sarcophagi of Emperor Constantine and his sainted mother, Helena. When collecting relics became a highly lucrative hobby, early Christian tombs like these were ransacked for the bones, shrouds and trinkets inside.

7 Head upstairs and through the Hall of the Candelabra, the Hall of Tapestries and the Hall of Maps.

The Hall of the Candelabra demonstrates the vastness of the Vatican collection – look out for the big toe below the first candlestick on your right. The Hall of Tapestries is decorated with 17th-century tapestries made with wool, silk, gold and silver threads. The Hall of Maps is covered with frescos of maps created by Ignazio Danti in the late 16th century.

8 At the very end of the corridor, turn left into the Sobieski Room and continue through the Room of the Immaculate Conception, around the outside corridor to the far end of the Raphael Rooms.

The four Raphael Rooms were intended to be Pope Julius II's private apartments. The first of these is the Room of Constantine, a banquet hall decorated with scenes from the life of Emperor Constantine, who granted religious freedom to Christians in AD 315. The Room of Heliodoros was Julius II's bedroom; the theme is the salvation of the church. The Room of the Papal Seal is home to what is considered Raphael's greatest masterpiece, *The School of Athens*. At its centre stand the fathers of philosophy, Plato and Aristotle. Look for the pleasant face of Raphael himself, just visible on the bottom right, looking out at you. The Room of the Fire in the Borgo is the last Raphael Room. Pope Leo X oversaw its decoration in 1514.

9 Leave the Raphael Rooms. Follow the signs to the Sistine Chapel.

The Sistine Chapel is named for Pope Sixtus IV, who commissioned its construction in 1471. New popes are elected here. Early Renaissance painters, including Sandro Botticelli and Pietro Perugino, painted the walls in 1481–82. Michelangelo painted the ceiling between 1508 and 1512. He returned again in 1536, at 61 years of age, to paint *The Last Judgment* on the altar wall. By this time he was known as *Il Divino*, Divine One. The ceiling was a huge undertaking for Michelangelo, who was not an experienced fresco painter. Three stories from the Book of Genesis (Creation of the Universe, Creation of Man and the Life of Noah) are told in nine scenes. Contrary to popular belief, he did not paint lying on his back, but standing. Michelangelo's work greatly impressed his fellow artists, but they all agreed that he painted like a sculptor.

10 Leave the chapel through the back right exit, which will take you into St Peter's church.

St Peter's Basilica was built in AD 326 on the site of an ancient pagan necropolis. This early church was demolished under Pope Julius II and a new cornerstone set in place in 1506 by architect Donato Bramante. Michelangelo designed the dome and Bernini executed much of the bronze and marble sculpture. The largest Christian basilica in the world, it is home to Michelangelo's *Pietà*, his first commission and the only work he ever signed. He made it in 1499 when he was 24 and at the start of his career.

11 The walk ends here. You can return to Ottaviano Metro station or take bus 23, 271 or 280 from the end of Via della Conciliazione.

13

Days of Plague in the Borgo

The Borgo district around the Vatican was once a centre of pilgrimage. Its name, from the Latin *burgus* meaning castle, refers to Castel Sant'Angelo.

Pope Leo IV built walls around the Borgo during the 9th century to protect the area from invaders. The area became known as the Civitas Leonina, a notoriously overcrowded city within a city. During the dangerous days of the Middle Ages, the protection offered by the fortification and castle attracted people from all over – including Saxons, Langobards and Franks from northern Europe. In the 1527 Sack of Rome, the Borgo district was particularly devastated. In later times it received an unfortunate makeover by Mussolini, who tried to modernize the city. Before this 1936 'urban renewal', visitors wound their way through dark medieval streets; you can still experience these back streets if you know where to go. The Castel Sant'Angelo, now a museum, looks out over the Borgo district. It has historically served as the mausoleum of Hadrian, Rome's only fortress and the pope's place of refuge during times of trouble. The popes made it more comfortable in the 14th century, with lavish rooms and new frescos. Today it's a good place to bring children, who enjoy exploring its dark passages.

1 Take bus 23, 64 or 280 to Piazza della Rovere.

The piazza is named for the Florentine family della Rovere, whose name means 'of the oak'. Both Pope Sixtus IV, who commissioned the construction of the Sistine Chapel, and Julius II, who commissioned the Sistine Chapel ceiling, were family members.

2 Walk through the arch of Porta Santo Spirito.

Porta Santo Spirito was built by Antonio da San Gallo and Michelangelo. The two friends argued about the best way to fortify the walls of the Borgo and, as a result, the project was never finished. Antonio da San Gallo never forgave Michelangelo's stubbornness.

3 Walk down Via dei Penitenzieri. Turn right on Borgo Santo Spirito.

The Santo Spirito complex on the right was built and endowed by Pope Innocent III in 1198 as a hospital and hostel for the poor. Look for the 16th-century *ruota degli esposti* (literally 'the wheel of the abandoned'). This revolving door allowed mothers to leave unwanted babies anonymously in the care of the church. Such children would have a double cross printed on their left foot and be registered as *filius matris ignotae* or 'child of unknown mother' – the origin of the Italian insult *figlio di mignotta*. During the Sack of Rome, troops stormed the hostel and murdered the orphans and pilgrims.

WHERE TO EAT

🍴 PIZZERIA VECCHIO,
Borgo Pio 27/a;
Tel: 06 68806355.
Great place to stop for a quick piece of pizza *al taglio,* sold by the slice.

🍴 LA VERANDA DELL'HOTEL COLUMBUS,
Borgo Santo Spirito 73;
Tel: 06 6872973.
Torch-lit courtyard, frescoed hall.

🍴 TRE PUPAZZI,
Borgo Pio 183, at Via dei Tre Pupazzi;
Tel: 06 68803220.
Well-priced trattoria, pleasant staff.

4 Turn left on Via Pio X and left again onto Via della Conciliazione.

Mussolini bulldozed two of the medieval streets from the Borgo district in order to build Via della Conciliazione (the Road of Reconciliation). The avenue was designed to celebrate the new feeling of accord in existence between the government and the Catholic Church. In fact, the road establishes a direct route from the Vatican to the centre of Rome, with a fine view of St Peter's. Santa Maria in Traspontina church at Via della Conciliazione 14 is a Carmelite church built to commemorate the soldiers who died while defending Castel Sant'Angelo during the Sack of Rome. The church was built on the site of an ancient Roman pyramid, thought during the

DISTANCE **1 mile (1.6km)**

ALLOW **2 hours**

START **Piazza della Rovere**

FINISH **Piazza Pia**

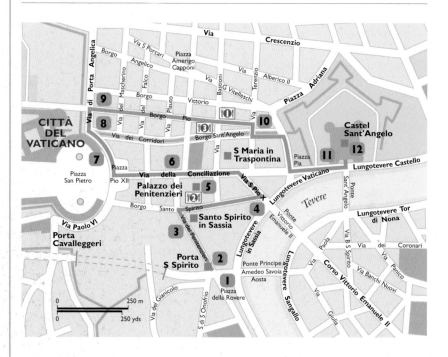

Middle Ages to be the tomb of Romulus, legendary founder of Rome.

5 Continue down the road to Via della Conciliazione 33.

The name of Palazzo dei Penitenzieri refers to the confessors of St Peter's who were once resident here. The palazzo was built in 1480 for Cardinal Domenico della Rovere, but it later passed into the possession of Cardinal Francesco Alidosi. He was a favourite of Pope Julius II della

Rovere, but was executed for treason in 1511. Today the building is used as a hotel – the Hotel Columbus.

6 Follow Via della Conciliazione to its culmination at Piazza San Pietro.

This grand piazza is often filled with pigeons and pilgrims. The travertine stone used for its 284 columns was plundered from the Coliseum. The bronze sphere on top of the obelisk was reputed to contain the ashes of Julius Caesar, but when

broken open it was empty. You can usually see the pope on Wednesday and Sunday mornings when he blesses devotees and travellers in the busy piazza.

7 Turn right through St Peter's Colonnade to Piazza Città Leonina.

From here you can admire the length of the *passetto* or passage that runs nearly half a mile (800m) from the Vatican palaces to Castel Sant'Angelo. This part of the Leonine wall was used as an escape route for the pope in times of danger. It was the route used by Clement VII Medici when he decided the time was right to flee during the 1527 Sack of Rome. As the pope fled to safety, a ragged and desperate band of Spanish, German and French troops, led by the Duke of Bourbon, massacred hundreds on St Peter's altar and burnt or destroyed countless church relics. Hundreds of others were drowned in the Tiber as crowds fled across bridges. Officers wielded no authority as soldiers raped, pillaged, tortured and murdered Romans. Witnesses told tales of victims branded with irons or forced to eat their own ears, noses or testicles as their tormentors compelled them to reveal the location of their most precious treasures. Those who survived the slaughter were prey to the plague from infected corpses. Pope Clement VII, blamed for his handling of the ordeal, died of fever in 1534. His tomb was smeared with dung and his funerary inscription *Clemens Pontifex*

Maximus was rewritten by vandals to read *InClemens Pontifex Maximus.*

8 Pass through the arches of Porta Angelica and walk down Via di Porta Angelica to Borgo Pio.

The point where Borgo Pio and Via di Porta Angelica meet is the only major traffic intersection in Vatican City, where residents and workers of the smallest country in the world can drive in and out. Swiss Guards direct the traffic. These young men are Swiss Catholics who must be celibate during their service.

9 Turn right down the lane known as Borgo Pio.

This lane is known for its seemingly endless array of restaurants, cafés and souvenir shops. Stop for coffee or lunch and watch the people go past.

10 Turn right at the end of Borgo Pio and cross left through the intersection of Piazza Pia on to Lungotevere Castello.

Ponte Sant'Angelo, across from the castle, is one of Rome's oldest bridges. Its three central arches are part of the original AD 138 bridge built as part of the triumphal route to Hadrian's funerary monument. It was reconstructed in 1668 and decorated with Bernini's sculpted angels, who are there to welcome and guide pilgrims toward St Peter's. Across the bridge once stood the infamous tower, Tor di Nona, a favoured spot for night-time torture

sessions and executions during the Inquisition. The artist Benvenuto Cellini was imprisoned there for sodomy.

11 Enter Castel Sant' Angelo on Lungotevere Castello.

Castel Sant'Angelo was originally the mausoleum of Emperor Hadrian, who died in AD 141. During the Middle Ages it became an infamous prison and dungeon. It was the site of military struggles in medieval Rome, as it was the only fortress in the city and was fought over by warring families and powers. In AD 590 Pope Gregory the Great led a march of penitents through the streets to pray for relief from an epidemic of the plague. Legend has it that the penitents saw Archangel Michael, guardian of the sick, sheathing his sword as a sign that the plague was coming to an end. From this moment it was known as Castel Sant'Angelo. Atop the castle stands a statue commemorating this miracle. The castle became the popes' fortress in 1277. Once inside the castle you can wind your way across the ramparts, through the dark passages and superbly frescoed halls, making your way to the upper terrace for a superb view of the city. Pay an extra fee to walk through the *passetto* and retrace the steps of history's unlucky popes, fleeing from danger.
CASTEL SANT' ANGELO; CLOSED MON.

12 You have finished the walk. You can take bus 23, 34, 271 or 280 from Piazza Pia at the end of Via della Conciliazione.

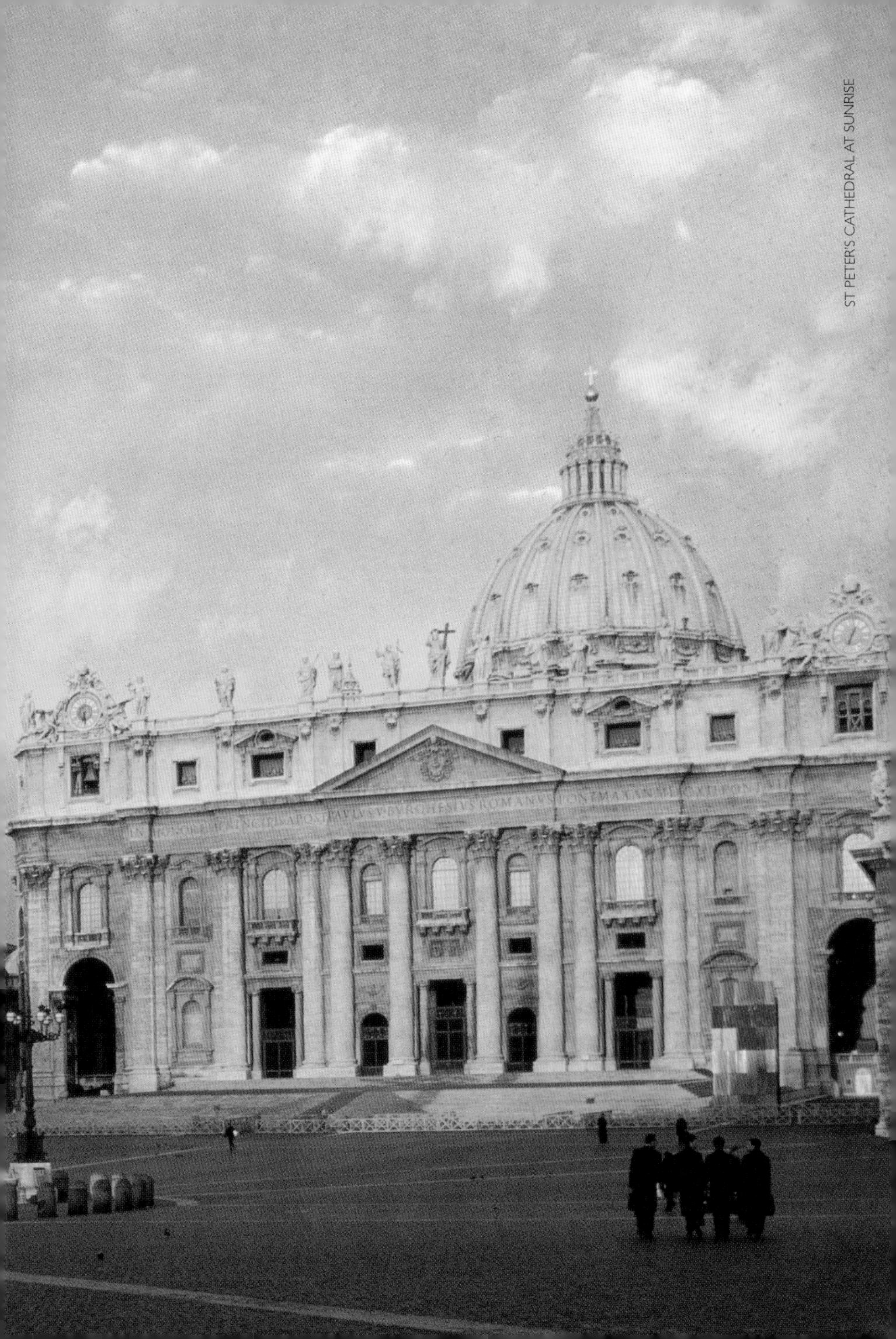

ST PETER'S CATHEDRAL AT SUNRISE

The Cradle of Romulus and Remus

This walk explores the heart of the ancient city that once ruled a mighty empire stretching all the way from Britain to Asia Minor.

The ancient Forum was the political, economic and religious centre of the Roman Empire. It was here that historic figures like Caesar spoke to crowds from the speaker's platform, argued in the courts of law and moulded the fate of modern Europe. As you follow the path of Via Sacra, or the Sacred Way, you walk in the footsteps of Rome's triumphant emperors as they returned victorious from campaigns, laden with treasure, slaves and glory for the *Senatus Populus Que Romanus,* Senate and People of Rome or SPQR. You will see this ancient stamp of the Roman Republic everywhere. The first Etruscan king drained this once marshy burial area in the 6th century BC by the construction of the Cloaca Maxima or great drain, which is still in use. The Forum lies in a valley between the Palatine and Capitoline Hills. With the decline of the empire, this area was forgotten, and by the Renaissance it was known as the *Campo Vaccino* or cow pasture! Not much more than the brick understructure is visible.

Take the Metro Line B to Colosseo station and you will surface in front of the Coliseum.

The Flavian Amphitheatre or Coliseum, the second-largest building in the ancient world after the Great Pyramid of Giza, was built in just eight years on the site of Emperor Nero's infamous Golden House. Nero was run out of Rome in AD 68 and subsequently forced to kill himself. He was succeeded by the popular general Flavius Vespasianus, who built the Coliseum as a symbolic gesture of his scorn for Nero's depraved and murderous behaviour. The Coliseum, built with spoils from Vespasian's recent pillaging in Jerusalem, was a gift from the emperor to the people. Emperor Titus celebrated its completion in AD 80 with 100 straight days of games and displays.

2 Cross Via dei Fori Imperiali and walk around to the right, where you will find the entrance to the Coliseum on Piazza del Colosseo.

From inside it is easy to see how much of the Coliseum was plundered by the popes to build their new Christian city. More than half of the outer wall is gone and the great marbles of the interior have been stripped away to reveal the most basic skeletal frame of this once-proud symbol of Roman imperial power. Below the reconstructed area of wooden flooring you can see backstage, where animals, gladiators and bits of scenery would be hidden from sight until the appropriate dramatic moment. Lift shafts

WHERE TO EAT

|O| LA PIAZZETTA,
Vicolo del Buon Consiglio 23a;
Tel: 06 6991640.
Well-located trattoria with particularly good desserts.

|O| OPPIO CAFFÉ,
Via delle Terme di Tito 72;
Tel: 06 4745262.
American restaurant and night club with a fabulous view of the Coliseum.
www.oppiocaffe.it

and passageways are clearly visible today. Make your way up the stairs to the top, which affords an excellent view.
COLISEUM: OPEN DAILY,
http://en.turismoroma.it

3 With the Coliseum behind you and the Arco di Costantino on your left, walk up Via Sacra, or the Sacred Way, to the Arco di Tito.

The Arch of Constantine in front of the Coliseum commemorates Emperor Constantine's victory over his rival for power at the Battle of the Milvian Bridge. It represents Constantine's successful efforts to reunite a divided empire under his sole control. Constantine reused artwork from the monuments of Emperors Trajan, Hadrian and Marcus Aurelius in order to associate himself with these so-called good emperors. As you walk up the hill to the Arch of Titus, you are walking on the oldest road

OPPOSITE: THE COLISEUM INTERIOR

23

DISTANCE **1 mile (1.6km)**

ALLOW **3 hours**

START **Colosseo Metro**

FINISH **Colosseo Metro or Piazza Venezia**

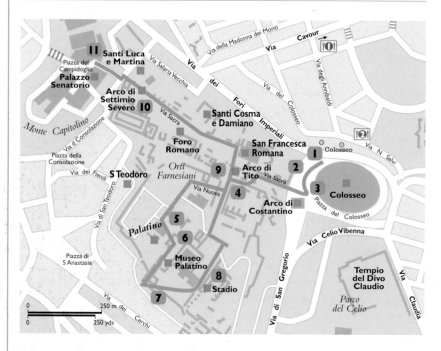

in Rome. On your right runs a length of wall from one side of the largest temple in Rome, dedicated to the two goddesses, Venus and Roma. At the top of the hill stands the Arch of Titus, built in AD 81 to commemorate Emperor Titus and his part in the Sack of Jerusalem that took place in AD 72. The fine reliefs beneath this arch depict a triumphant Emperor Titus, resplendent in his chariot, alongside a procession of Jewish slaves who are carrying looted treasures from the Temple of Herod back to Rome.

4 Turn left at the Arco di Tito and turn right along Via Nuova. Climb the stairs on the left up through the Farnese grottos, past the aviaries and onto the Palatine Hill.

In the 16th century the Palatine Hill became the site of a large villa belonging to the Farnese family, whose wealth and aristocratic prestige came from generations of military service to the popes. These stairs, fountains and grottoes were part of this extensive villa. At the

top of the hill stand two aviaries, where exotic birds were kept, and the Farnese gardens, filled with orange groves, stretch before you. The Palatine Hill is the first of the Seven Hills of Rome. Recent archaeological excavations here have brought to light settlements from as early as the 10th century BC. The English word 'palace' is derived from Palatine: the palaces of the emperors eventually stretched across the expanse of this hill.

5 Turn left at the first opportunity and then continue straight ahead.

When you reach a clearing on the other side of the gardens, notice the brick ruins to your immediate left. These constitute what remains of the Domus Flavia, a complex of palaces dating back to the 1st century AD and named for the Flavian dynasty. Some suspect that Emperor Titus's younger brother, Domitian, poisoned him to claim the throne. Justice caught up with him in this garden, where assassins stabbed him to death. A large courtyard stood at the centre of the palace and the base of its octagonal fountain is still visible.

6 Pass through this courtyard towards the Palatine Museum, which stands at the centre of the hill. Turn right past the museum to the back of the hill.

The Palatine Museum holds some of the hill's more fragile archaeological finds. Wall paintings, stucco and graceful statuary from the Temple of Apollo can be found inside. At the back of the

Palatine Hill you get an extensive view over the Circus Maximus. From this vantage point the emperor could enjoy races and games from his private box. Look down into the sunken gardens of the Domus Augustana: this private sphere of the palace complex was accessible only to the emperor and his closest associates. **PALATINE MUSEUM**; OPEN TUE-SUN; www.archeorm.arti.beniculturali.it

7 Facing the back of the museum, turn right and weave your way through the ruins of the Domus Augustana to the sunken hippodrome.

The large Stadium of Domitian lies on the eastern side of the Palatine Hill. Horses were probably raced in the elliptical area to the right. You can also spot the remains of the emperor's grandstand opposite you, where he enjoyed private entertainments.

8 Walk down the length of the Stadium of Domitian and turn left at the farthest end of the ruins. Make your way down the hill along the paving stones that lead back to the Arco di Tito. From the Arco di Tito you can continue your descent along Via Sacra into the central square or Forum.

On your right, admire the massive monolithic columns of the Temple of Faustina and Antoninus Pius. This temple was first dedicated to the deified wife of Pius in AD 141, but after his death they were enshrined together. Legend has it that this was the site of St Laurence's

gruesome martyrdom, where he was grilled to death. Across from the Temple of Faustina and Antoninus Pius, below the ruins of the Palatine palaces, are the Temple and House of the Vestal Virgins. The six Vestal Virgins of Rome were well respected; the only women of rank in ancient Roman society. These women devoted their lives to chastity and the Goddess of the hearth, Vesta.

9 Continue down Via Sacra to the back of the Forum, where the Arco di Settimio Severo looms.

At the back of the Forum stands the triumphal arch of Septimius Severus. This celebrates the tenth anniversary of the reign of the first African emperor and his conquests over the Arabs and Parthians. To the right of the arch rises the Curia or senate house. The first was built in 52 BC, but the current building dates from AD 283, when it was rebuilt after a fire. Clap your hands when inside to hear the amazing acoustics. To the left of the arch of Septimius Severus is a low-lying wall,

the Rostra, where the greatest orators of Rome made political announcements. Cicero's eloquent opposition to Caesar's growing power inevitably led to his execution in 43 BC. Apparently, his head was then mounted on the Rostra, where Mark Antony's wife plunged her hairpin through his tongue.

10 Pass underneath the Arco di Settimio Severo.

Behind the arch is the back of the Palazzo Senatorio. From this side you can see the various architectural substructures that support the 16th-century palace. The arches at the lower level are part of the 1st-century BC Tabularium or record-keeping office of the ancient world, while a fortified medieval tower is visible on the right side of the edifice.

11 Leave the Forum on the north side and turn right down Via dei Fori Imperiali back to the Colosseo Metro station or turn left and head to Piazza Venezia and the city centre.

27

Peaceful Places
of the Aventine

The Aventine is one of the Seven Hills of Rome. Today it is a peaceful residential district of the city, full of lovely gardens and churches.

The Aventine hill lies on the southern side of Rome. During the 5th century BC, and throughout the Republic, the area was occupied by the lower plebeian classes of Rome with their densely populated homes, but during the imperial period it became a favourite residential district for Rome's elite patrician class. It was integrated into the city by Emperor Claudius (AD 41–54) and became a lively business quarter because of its proximity to the harbour on the river. In fact, the nearby Montetestaccio is a 118ft (36m) high mound of broken amphorae used to transport wine and oil. The Goths sacked the city in the 5th century and plundered the luxurious villas. Today the elegant district offers an escape from the busy streets of central Rome. It remains a high class area with some enviable grand houses, medieval churches and public parks.

1 Take Metro line B to Piramide or take bus 23, 280 or 30. Leave the station in the direction of Via Ostiense. Cross Via Ostiense to reach the very visible pyramid.

In front of you stand parts of the impressive Aurelian walls of the city, built to defend Rome from attack. On your right is the Porta San Paolo, one of 18 original gates. The Pyramid of Caius Cestius was incorporated into the walls. This monument was built in 12 BC to inter the remains of a very wealthy praetor (a chief magistrate), who had a taste for Egyptian architecture in common with many of his peers during the Golden Age of Augustan Rome.

2 Pass between Porta San Paolo and the Pyramid, heading on to Via Marmorata, then turn left onto Via Caio Cestio. The entrance to the Protestant Cemetery is a short way down on the left at No. 6.

Until the late 18th century non-Catholics, with the exception of Jews, were not permitted to be buried in Rome. This Protestant burial ground was created around 1821 and is the Père-Lachaise of Rome. Here lie the remains of the Romantic poets John Keats and Percy Bysshe Shelley, Goethe's illegitimate son, Julius Augustus, and Antonio Gramsci, first leader of the Italian communist party. Shelley's young son was also buried here and the poet commented that the beauty of this place 'might make one in love with death'.

PROTESTANT CEMETERY; CLOSED WED, DONATIONS APPRECIATED.

3 Leave the cemetery heading back to Via Marmorata and turn left. You will pass one of the city's major post offices. At the major intersection of Via Galvani, cross the street and head up the hill on Via Pollione.

Nearing the end of Via Porta Lavernale on the left is Sant'Anselmo. This modern church has a beautiful little courtyard worth exploring. Every Sunday during Mass (8.30am) or Vespers (7.45pm) you can enjoy the solemn Gregorian chants.

DISTANCE 1 mile (1.6km)

ALLOW 1.5 hours

START **Piramide Metro**

FINISH **Circo Massimo Metro**

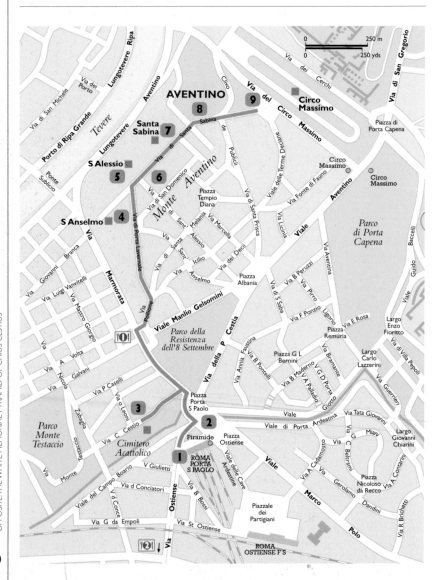

OPPOSITE: THE WHITE MEMORIAL PYRAMID OF CAIUS CESTIUS

4 Proceed down Via Pollione then Via di Porta Lavernale to Piazza Cavalieri di Malta.

The large green doorway of No. 3 is surmounted by the symbolic cross of the Knights of Malta, also known as the Knights Hospitaller, an organization that began as a hospital founded in Jerusalem in 1080 to provide care for poor and sick pilgrims to the Holy Land. If you look through the keyhole you will see a stunning view of St Peter's dome framed by the gardens. Giovanni Battista Piranese designed the enclosure in 1765.

5 Turn right down Via di S. Sabina and come to Santi Bonifacio e Alessio.

This church, dedicated to two early Christian martyrs, was built prior to the 10th century and rebuilt in 1750. St Alexis (Alessio) was the son of a senator. He went on a pilgrimage to the Orient in order to evade an arranged marriage.

6 Go down Via di S. Sabina to Santa Sabina on Piazza Pietro d'Illiria.

Santa Sabina is the gem of the Aventine. This basilica, founded in AD 425 by

Pietro d'Illiria over the house of a wealthy Roman matron who was martyred by the sword, is one of the best preserved early churches in Rome. The wooden doors of the vestibule are made from cypress wood and are among the oldest wooden reliefs of early Christian times. If you look at the top left panel you will see one of the earliest images of a crucifixion. Early Christian iconography avoided the subject of the Passion as these events were thought to reveal Christ's weakness and humanity, and this image avoids any reference to gore or the agony of Christ's suffering.

WHERE TO EAT

🍴 **TUTTI FRUTTI,**
Via Luca della Robbia 3/a;
Tel: 06 5757902.
Booking advisable. All the ingredients are fresh from the market so the menu changes daily. Special seafood menu on Fridays.

🍷 **DOPPIOZEROO,**
Via Ostiense 68;
Tel: 06 57301961.
Hip wine bar and restaurant.

7 Leaving Santa Sabina, pass through Piazza Pietro d'Illiria into the Orange Gardens of Parco Savello.

There is a lovely fountain in the piazza and splendid views of Rome and St Peter's basilica from the orange gardens. This is a perfect place to stop for a picnic lunch or sit and savour the moment.

8 Set off once again down Via di S. Sabina, which soon becomes Via Valle Murcia.

You will emerge into the Rose Gardens that were planted on the site of the first Jewish cemetery in Rome. During May, the gardens are open for the annual rose-growing competition.

9 The walk ends here. You can turn right on Via del Circo Massimo and continue to the Circo Massimo Metro at the end of the street.

OVERLEAF: CHURCH OF SAN CLEMENTE

Old Papal Stomping Grounds

Explore the Lateran district, where the popes lived for a thousand years, and discover the often-overlooked gems of early Christian Rome.

This walk explores the origins of the papacy. Its long and eventful history begins at the Lateran palace, where the popes lived for centuries before moving to the Vatican in the 14th century. Once owned by the wealthy Laterani family, this area was presented to Emperor Constantine as part of his wife's dowry. It seems that Constantine then gave the site to the popes in AD 312 so that they could build a church. Constantine supported Christian building projects, but because he didn't want to offend powerful pagan aristocrats, he kept this new religion on the margins of the city. San Giovanni in Laterano, the church of St John, is in fact the official *cathedra* or seat of the popes and the earliest church building in the city. St John and Santa Croce are two of the seven major pilgrimage churches of Rome.

Take Metro Line B to Colosseo station (or Bus 85, 87 to Piazza San Clemente). From Colosseo, turn left and walk up Via di San Giovanni in Laterano to Piazza di San Clemente.

San Clemente is one of 28 titular churches in Rome known to have existed as early as the 3rd century. It is named after St Clement, the third Roman bishop or pope after St Peter. According to legend, he was thrown into the Black Sea with an anchor tied to his feet. The church was burnt to the ground by Norman invaders in 1084, but reconstructed on higher ground in the early 12th century. San Clemente offers a unique example of Rome's many layers. You can descend into the bowels of the church to the original 1st-century Roman houses, which were destroyed in the famous fire of AD 64 during the reign of Nero. Here you will also see a well-preserved 2nd-century Mithraeum. The mysterious cult of Mithras, originally from Persia and particularly important for Roman legionaries, once performed their rituals here. Rivalry between Christianity and Mithras was fierce in the 3rd century. Christian opponents of the cult even accused its members of ritual child murder, though modern scholars have proved that the cult mainly worshipped the stars. One level above, you can admire the Romanesque wall paintings of the early church that mainly depict events in the life of St Clement. Finally emerging into the light of the upper 12th-century church, you can enjoy the beautiful apse mosaic and the Chapel of St Catherine.

WHERE TO EAT

🍽 ALCHEMILLA,
Via di San Giovanni in Laterano 220;
Tel: 06 77203202.
7-course meals a speciality.

🍽 BUONI AMICI,
Via Aleardo Aleardi 4;
Tel: 06 70491993.
Pizzeria just off Piazza San Giovanni.

🍽 DOME ROCK CAFÉ,
Via D. Fontana 18; Tel: 06 70452436.
Trendy pub with live music.

The paintings within this chapel by Florentine painters Masolino and Masaccio are the earliest example of Renaissance painting in the city of Rome. The beautiful choir screen was salvaged from the earlier 6th-century construction. Today the church is administered by Irish Dominicans.

2 Leave the church and turn left, continuing down Via di San Giovanni in Laterano briefly. Turn right on Via dei Querceti and then turn immediately left on to Via dei Santi Quattro Coronati. The church of Santi Quattro Coronati is on your right.

This 4th-century church is named for four Roman soldiers, Christian martyrs who were crowned with wreaths of iron spikes that were driven into their skulls. Like San Clemente, the church was destroyed during the Norman invasions

OPPOSITE: MITHRAIC TEMPLE BELOW CHURCH OF SAN CLEMENTE

37

DISTANCE **1.5 miles (2.4km)**

ALLOW **2 hours**

START **Colosseo Metro**

FINISH **San Giovanni Metro**

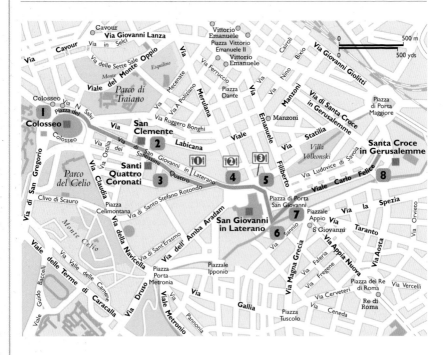

and rebuilt in the 12th century. The harsh exterior shows that it became part of military fortifications surrounding the Lateran palaces a hundred years later. Today it is attached to a convent for Augustinian nuns. The small oratory of St Sylvester contains a series of political frescos from the 13th century, which depict the mythical conversion and baptism of Emperor Constantine and his subsequent submission to the papacy in Rome. These images are assertions of the pope's power, intended to shame and criticize Emperor Fredrick II for daring to contest this divine authority.

3 Continue down Via dei San Quattro Coronati. Turn left on to Via di Santo Stefano Rotondo and merge right on to Via San Giovanni in Laterano, which will lead you to Piazza di San Giovanni in Laterano and the Baptistery.

The large palace complex you see today is a 16th-century construction by Domenico Fontana. The obelisk in the

CHRISTO · SALVATORI ·

piazza was brought to Rome in AD 357 from the Temple of Ammon in Thebes and dates to 1500 BC. The Baptistery can be entered from Piazza di San Giovanni in Laterano. It has a beautiful ceiling mosaic depicting the Lamb of God at its apex, thought to have been created in the 5th century. The green basalt font dates back to classical antiquity.

BAPTISTERY;
OPEN DAILY EXCEPT LUNCHTIME

4 Leave the Baptistery and turn right. Cross the piazza and the street to the Scala Santa or Holy Staircase.

The Holy Staircase of 28 steps was brought from Pontius Pilate's palace in Jerusalem by Constantine's mother St Helena and is said to have been scaled by Christ shortly before his death. Even today, pilgrims often mount the steps upon their knees in order to replicate a fraction of Christ's sufferings.

SCALA SANTA;
OPEN DAILY EXCEPT LUNCHTIME

5 Leave the Scala Santa and turn left. Cross the street once again to Piazza di Porta San Giovanni, where you can go inside the church of San Giovanni in Laterano.

San Giovanni in Laterano (St John in the Lateran) is known as 'Mother and head of all churches in the city and on earth'.

SAN GIOVANNI IN LATERANO

Inside, large statues of the 12 apostles line the nave. The Papal Altar was sculpted by Giovanni di Stefano in the 14th century. Only the pope may give Mass at the altar, which is said to contain the wooden table upon which the first bishops of Rome celebrated Mass. On the upper part of this beautiful altar are busts of St Peter and Paul in silver gilt. Don't miss the 13th-century cloister with its barley-sugar-striped, mosaic-encrusted columns.

6 Leave the church and walk straight across Piazza di Porta San Giovanni.

Passing under the arches of Porta San Giovanni to the piazza you will see the monument (1927) to St Francis of Assisi. Pope Gregory XIII had this entrance inserted into the Aurelian walls by Iacopo del Duca in 1574, to make life easier for pilgrims heading from San Giovanni to Santa Croce. Gregory XIII is responsible for the Gregorian calendar we use today. Inspired by Protestant-Catholic antipathy and reformative zeal, Gregory XIII is also remembered for his cruel celebrations of the St Bartholomew massacre of the Huguenots in France.

7 Cross the intersection and walk down Viale Carlo Felice to Piazza Santa Croce in Gerusalemme.

Santa Croce is named for the Holy Cross that was supposedly recovered by St Helena, Constantine's mother, on her journey to the Holy Land in AD 326. It is the most precious relic of the church. Emperor Constantine had this church

COLUMNS WITH MOSAICS AT SAN GIOVANNI

built over his mother's palaces at the end of the 4th century. Its 18th-century appearance is attributed to the pontificate of Benedict XIV, a man well respected for his intelligence, moderation and engaging manners. Benedict XIV was also responsible for introducing the first street signs into Rome – he had a predilection for wandering off into far-flung corners of the city, in disguise, in order to attend to parishioners. It is thought that he may have lost his way a few times and decided that street signs seemed like a good idea.

8 The walk ends here. Return to Metro Line A San Giovanni station.

41

The Devil's District: Trastevere

Trastevere's dark alleys and narrow cobbled streets once ran with blood from the butchers and tanning shops, and were lit by ghostly lamplight.

Trastevere lies on the west bank of the Tiber and is the oldest preserved district in the city. The name literally means 'across the Tiber'. During the Middle Ages this district of the city was occupied mostly by foreigners. The residents flung their rubbish and excrement into the dirty, cramped streets and it was a scary and threatening place to wander in at night. Today Trastevere is famous for its picturesque ivy-covered alleys, good restaurants and summer street performers. It is an area where you will hear Roman dialect and get a feel for genuine Roman ways. Old people sit out in the street and you will enjoy the colourful laundry displays that hang across the alleys above your head. It is best to take this walk in the early evening. At dusk, performers fill the piazzas with music and Rome's eclectic community walks, chats and celebrates being alive.

1 Take bus 23, 271 or 280 to begin the walk at Ponte Sisto.

Pope Sixtus IV built Ponte Sisto over the Tiber (or Tevere) in preparation for the 1475 Holy Year. While workers laid the cornerstone, the pope dropped gold coins into the river as a blessing. There is a wonderful view of St Peter's dome from the bridge. If you have not already done so, cross the bridge to Trastevere. On the left bank, Piazza Trilussa is named after a Roman poet and marked by a fountain that has become a meeting place; the focus of bohemian life in this area.

2 Turn left down Via della Renella, right on Vicolo Santa Rufina and left again on Via della Lungaretta to Piazza Sonnino.

At Via della Lungaretta you will see the modest church of St Agatha. This saint is known for having devoted her life to Christianity from a very young age. She was martyred by horrific forms of torture at the age of 15.

3 Turn right on Viale di Trastevere to San Crisogono at Piazza Sonnino 44.

San Crisogono is a 5th-century church that was largely rebuilt in 1626, but its Romanesque *campanile* or bell tower dates to 1125. Excavations have revealed that San Crisogono was one of 25 5th-century *titulus* churches. In the earliest years of Christianity, the cardinal priests took their titles from these churches. San Crisogono is decorated with a spectacular apse mosaic and has superb Cosmati marble floors.

4 Turn left down Via VII Coorte to Caserma dei Vigili della VII Coorte.

On the left-hand side of this small side street are the ruins of the barracks of an ancient fire brigade, Caserma dei Vigili della VII Coorte, manned by the seventh cohort of the Roman military. It was constructed under Augustus in the 1st century. Like most of the treasures of the city, you need to book to visit this site. **CASERMA DEI VIGILI DELLA VII COORTE;** OPEN ON REQUEST, TEL: 06 67103819

5 Turn right and immediately left down Via Santini, which becomes Via dei Genovesi. Turn left a few feet down Vicolo dell Atleta.

On the left you will see the lovely portico and façade of a house that once

DISTANCE 1.5 miles (2.4km)

ALLOW 2 hours

START Ponte Sisto

FINISH Lungotevere della Farnesina

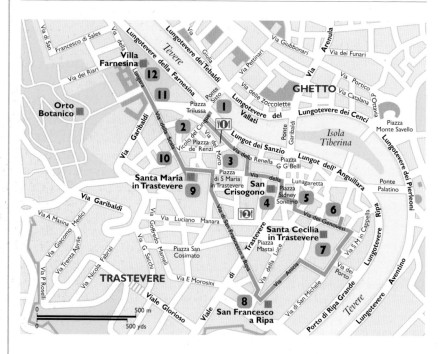

concealed the oldest synagogue in the city. The name of this small street is taken from an important archaeological find. A 1st-century BC marble statue of an athlete (now in the antique galleries of the Vatican Museums) was discovered just a few feet away. This statue was actually a Roman copy of a famous Greek statue, *Apoxyomenos*, by the artist Lysippus, cast in bronze during the 4th century BC. It depicts a wrestler cleaning the slippery wax from his limbs before climbing into the public baths.

6 Walk back to Via dei Genovesi and continue to the left. Turn right on Via di Santa Cecilia to reach Piazza di Santa Cecilia.

The church of Santa Cecilia was built in the 5th century over the house of a wealthy Roman woman who was named after the Christian martyr, St Cecilia. Pope Paschal I then transported the saint's tomb here from the catacombs in the 9th century. St Cecilia was sentenced to die by suffocation in the steam of her

WHERE TO EAT

🍴 **LA RENELLA,**
Via del Moro 15-16;
Tel: 06 5817265.
This wonderfully fragrant bakery at the heart of Trastevere serves pizza, bread and pastries. When it is busy, take a number.

🍴 **PIZZERIA POPI-POPI,**
Via delle Fratte di Trastevere 45;
Tel: 06 5895167.
Delicious, well-priced pizza with tables outside.

bathroom in AD 230, but survived both this and attempts by a Roman soldier to decapitate her. She then lingered in her prison cell, singing hymns to God, before dying of her wounds three days later. St Cecilia later became the patron saint of musicians. Under the altar you can see a sculpture of her tortured body by Stefano Maderno (1600). Legend has it that he sculpted her body exactly as it was found in her tomb when it was opened in 1599. Also inside the church are rare medieval painting masterpieces by Pietro Cavallini dating to the 13th century.

7 Continue down Via di San Michele and turn right on Via della Madonna dell'Orto. Turn left on Via Anicia to Piazza di San Francesco a Ripa.

The church of Francesco a Ripa was built in the 17th century over what was once San Biagio hostel for pilgrims,

where St Francis of Assisi is said to have slept when he came to Rome in 1219. Inside is one of Gianlorenzo Bernini's most notable masterpieces, *Blessed Ludovica Albertoni* (1674), in the Altieri Chapel. This fine example of his theatrical Baroque style was done while he was in his mid-seventies.

8 Turn right down Via di San Francesco a Ripa to Piazza di Santa Maria in Trastevere.

You are now at the heart of Trastevere. The oldest church dedicated to the Virgin Mary stands here. Oil sprang from the ground on this spot in 38 BC and it was taken as a sign of the coming of the Saviour. The current construction dates from the 12th century and replaced an earlier 4th-century church that once stood here. Antique columns line the nave and stunning 12th-century gold mosaics decorate the apse. Outside under the portico, take note of the fragments of early Christian carvings and symbols. See if you can spot the anchor, an early Christian symbol of the role religious faith can play in a troubled life.

9 At Piazza di Santa Maria in Trastevere, turn left down Via della Lungaretta and right down Via della Scala to Piazza di Sant'Egidio.

The church of Sant'Egidio was built in 1630 as a centre to help the poor and needy. Next door, the Roma in Trastevere Museum houses a collection of engravings and paintings from the 18th and 19th centuries that capture the atmosphere of Roman life during that period. In the evenings this square is filled with street artists and musicians.

TRASTEVERE MUSEUM; OPEN TUE-SUN

10 Head straight down Via della Scala to reach the corner of Via Garibaldi.

The house on the corner of Via di Santa Dorotea and Via di Porta Settimiana was once the residence of Raphael's famous model and mistress, La Fornarina – the baker's daughter. She is thought to have been Margherita, daughter of a Sienese baker who lived and worked here at No. 20 Via di Santa Dorotea. Raphael probably met her while painting in the Villa Farnesina next door. Learning of his imminent death in 1520, the painter shunned her and forbade her to attend his funeral ceremony. Four months later she took her vows at a local convent. Raphael immortalized her face in a portrait, *La Fornarina* (1519), which can be seen at Palazzo Barberini: the love-struck artist signed his name on her arm as if to claim her as his own.

11 Pass under the Porta Settimiana down Via della Lungara to Villa Farnesina on Via della Lungaretta 230.

This villa is named after the Farnese family who acquired it in 1577. However, it was originally built for the Sienese banker, Agostino Chigi, who was the richest man in Europe at the time. He financed Popes Julius II and Leo X.

Between 1507 and 11 he hired architect Baldassare Peruzzi to design his palace. Chigi held lavish entertainments that included throwing silverware into the Tiber as a display of opulence. Raphael, Sebastiano del Piombo, Sodoma and Peruzzi painted the sumptuous frescos. There is a scene devoted to *Cupid and Psyche* (1517), celebrating love, in honour of the banker's pending marriage to his mistress, with whom he already had four children. The fruit and vegetables in the border have erotic overtones.

VILLA FARNESINA, OPEN MON-SAT 9-1

12 The walk ends here. Bus 23, 271 or 280 runs from Lungotevere.

Rome at Your Feet

**The Janiculum Hill is one of Rome's most peaceful places, with a
180-degree panoramic view of the Eternal City at its summit.**

This walk takes you to the top of the Janiculum hill, not one of the Seven Hills
of Rome – it's well outside the ancient cityscape – but the highest hill nearby.
Its name derives from the Latin *iani collis*, meaning hill of Janus, after the god of
gateways, beginnings and endings, and refers to its ancient location at the edge
of Rome. As you climb, pause to enjoy the views of the city from different
vantage points. This area played an important part in Rome's modern history
when the fighters of the Roman Republic defended themselves against French
troops summoned to assist Pope Pius IX in his claims over Rome. Today it
encompasses an elite residential district known as Monteverde. Homeowners
here have spectacular views over the city and pay substantially for the privilege.
Monteverde means 'green mountain' and indeed the district is known for its
tree-lined avenues and parks, like villa pamphili and villa sciarra.

Take bus 23, 115, 271 or 280 to Lungotevere Farnesina or Via Garibaldi. Make your way to Via della Lungara and turn left on Via Corsini to Largo Cristina di Svezia and Palazzo Corsini at Via della Lungara 10.

Palazzo Corsini, on the right corner of Via Corsini, was originally Palazzo Riario, built in the 16th century. Erasmus, Bramante and Michelangelo lived here, as did Queen Christina of Sweden, one of Rome's most eccentric residents, until her death in 1689. Aged 27, Queen Christina abdicated her throne and embraced the Roman Catholic Church. She moved to Rome and shocked the elite with her outrageous exploits. She wore men's clothing, fell in love with nuns and cardinals alike, and once introduced her friend, Ebba, to the British ambassador as her 'bedfellow'. Pope Alexander VII described her as 'a woman born a barbarian, barbarously brought up and having barbarous thoughts'. Despite this scandalous behaviour, she is buried in St Peter's. Palazzo Riario became Palazzo Corsini when it was rebuilt by the Corsini family in 1732. Today it houses a museum of art.

PALAZZO CORSINI;
OPEN MON-SAT 8.30-1.45

2 Enter the Botanical Gardens at Largo Cristina di Svezia No. 24.

Palazzo Riario was famed for its grand and lovely gardens. During her residence, Queen Christina continued to enrich the grounds, spending lavishly on fruit trees and exotic flowers. Today the 12 hectares of botanical gardens belong to the university of Rome: 7,000 different plant species from around the world grow here.

BOTANICAL GARDENS; OPEN DAILY

3 Leave the gardens and turn right on Via della Lungara and right again on Via Garibaldi, which winds up to Piazza San Pietro in Montorio.

DISTANCE **1.5 miles (2.4km)**

TIME **2.5 hours**

START **Lungotevere della Farnesina or Via Garibaldi**

FINISH **Largo Porta San Pancrazio**

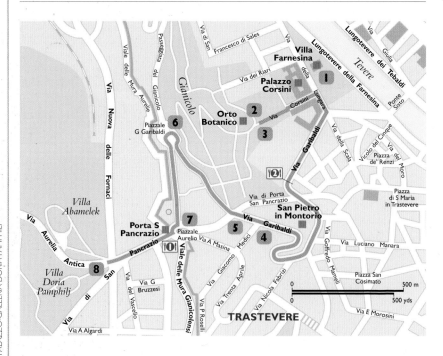

The church of San Pietro in Montorio was originally built before the 9th century on the site where it was erroneously believed St Peter had been crucified. Ferdinand and Isabella of Spain financed its rebuilding in the 1480s. Sebastiano del Piombo's *Flagellation of Christ* (1518) can be admired in the first chapel on the right, Bernini (1598-1680) designed the second chapel on the right and Giorgio Vasari decorated the large chapel on the left. The church was badly damaged in 1849 during the fighting between Garibaldi's Unification forces and the French troops fighting for the Popes. The *Tempietto*, or small temple, in the church courtyard is considered the first truly Renaissance structure in the city. Donato Bramante, head architect of the Vatican and first architect of new St Peter's, was the man responsible for designing its perfect proportions.

4 Continue down Via Garibaldi to the Fonte Aqua Paola.

WHERE TO EAT

🍴 **ANTICO ARCO,**
Piazzale Aurelio 7;
Tel: 06 5815274.
Next to a busy road, this place has
great wines and a good atmosphere.

🍴 **ANTICA PESA,**
Via Garibaldi 18;
Tel: 06 5809236. www.anticapesa.it
Named after the papal tax office
located on Via Garibaldi in the
17th century.

Pope Paul V ordered the construction of
this majestic fountain overlooking the
city to celebrate the repair of an
important Roman aqueduct in 1612.
Emperor Trajan commissioned the
original in AD 109, but it was destroyed
by barbarian invaders in the Middle Ages.
After the repairs, the fountain was
renamed the Paola Aqueduct in honour
of Pope Paul V.

5 Turn right just after the fountain on
Via Aldo Fabrizi up to Piazzale G.
Garibaldi.

STATUE OF GARIBALDI ON THE TREE-LINED RIDGE OF THE GIANCOLO

When modern Italy was in its infancy, Rome posed the most serious obstacle to reunification. The popes were kings of Rome and had no desire to relinquish their temporal powers over the city. Italians had to fight the pope for their capital. At the centre of Piazza Garibaldi stands an equestrian monument erected in 1895 to Giuseppe Garibaldi (1807–1882), principal military leader of the Italian Unification. This revolutionary from Nice served as general of the first Italian troops. It was here that he and his men assured the survival of the new Italian Republic in 1849. Garibaldi, the son of a tailor who started his career as a sailor, was a talented guerilla leader. He returned to Italy in 1848 after time spent in South America, where he had fled after a previously unsuccessful insurrection for Italy. The young revolutionaries led by Garibaldi perhaps looked more like bandits than national heroes, with their long hair, matted beards and black hats. The Janiculum Hill was the site of fierce fighting between Garibaldi's forces and those in support of the pope. In fact, the monument proclaims, 'Roma o Morte… Rome or Death!' The spectacular view of the Eternal City from this piazza is best appreciated at sunrise and sunset.

6 Turn down the Passeggiata del Gianicolo to Largo Porta San Pancrazio.

The arch of Porta San Pancrazio you see today was built in 1854 after it was destroyed during the fighting between Italian republican troops and French forces who defended the pope at the time of Unification. It stands on the site of the ancient Porta Aurelia, one of the original 3rd-century entrances to the city through the Aurelian walls. The Via Aurelia, which stretches off beside Villa Doria Pamphilj before the archway, is also known as State Road No. 1. The road was built in the 3rd century AD by Consul Aurelio Cotta to connect Rome with the new provinces. It follows the coast all the way to France.

7 Turn right down Via di San Pancrazio until you come to the entrance of Villa Doria Pamphilj.

The Villa Doria Pamphili was the suburban residence of Prince Camillo Pamphilj, nephew of Pope Innocent X. The grounds and the palace within were built in the 17th century and now constitute the largest public park in the city. Walk through the villa to enjoy the beautiful sculpture gardens of the residential palace, Casino del Bel Respiro, and the fabulous fountains, orange trees and lakes. The park is a favourite destination for joggers, walkers and families. Outdoor concerts take place here during the summer and the park is open until dark. You might decide to take a picnic and spend some time in its pleasant surroundings.

8 The walk ends here. Buses 870 and 115 leave from Largo Porta San Pancrazio.

Rogues and Rascals

Explore Quirinal Hill through the lives of the bad guys – popes, princes and fools – who held the reins of Rome and caused mayhem in the city.

The Quirinal Hill takes its name from Quirinus, an early god of the Roman state. In ancient times this was a district of Roman villas and public bath complexes. It was largely rebuilt in the 16th century, when important palaces began to spring up along the wide streets. Now it is defined at its peak by the Palazzo Quirinal, which has served as a papal palace, residence of the king of Italy and now home of the President of the Republic. From this vantage point you can look out over the rooftops and see the dome of St Peter's. According to Roman legend, the Quirinal Hill was once home to a small village of the Sabine tribe, who erected an altar to the god Quirinal here. Quirinal was god of the peaceful activities of free men, and the name may come from the Latin *curia*, meaning senate. Yet among the legends of early Rome the Sabine tribe was assaulted by desperate Roman men seeking wives, and the famous Rape of the Sabines thus constitutes one of Rome's earliest acts of aggression.

> **1** Take bus 44, 46, 60 or 271 to start the walk at Piazza Venezia.

This square is named after 15th-century Palazzo Venezia, originally the Venetian embassy, but later the principal offices of Il Duce. Mussolini gave his most notorious and dramatic speeches from its balcony. According to locals he left lights burning through the night to give people the impression that he was working late for the glory of the *popolo*. The Duce organized aerial displays of the Italian airforce, ordering the same squadrons to pass by repeatedly to deceive the public into thinking that the Italian forces were infinite. Across the piazza on the corner of Via del Corso is the Palazzo Bonaparte, where Napoleon's mother lived from 1815 to 1836. When Napoleonic troops finally withdrew from the occupation of Rome in 1814, the pope was surprisingly forgiving towards his family, especially as he had run off with many of Rome's art treasures. The Vittoriano, which dominates the busy piazza, is a gigantic monument created to celebrate the new Italian Republic. Its central equestrian statue represents Vittorio Emanuel II, first king of Italy. His moustache is five feet wide! His dynasty did not last. Less than 100 years later the family was banned from the country for fascist collaboration.

> **2** Turn right on Via IV November. Cross the street and turn left through Piazza Santi Apostoli.

The first church of the Sainted Apostles was built here in the mid-6th century

under Pope Pelagius I. It was restored many times during the Renaissance by the most illustrious popes, members of the della Rovere, Medici and Colonna families. Its current neo-classical façade is the work of architect Giuseppe Valadier (1762-1839).

> **3** Turn right on Via del Vaccaro to Piazza della Pilotta and right on Via della Pilotta. Palazzo Colonna can be found at No. 17.

This piazza and the adjacent street get their name from a sort of ball game that was played here after the Sack of Rome in 1527. It consisted of hitting a makeshift ball with a spoon or bare fist against the wall – desperate times call for desperate games. The four arches above Via della Pilotta are actually footbridges that connect Palazzo Colonna with its

DISTANCE **1 mile (1.6km)**

ALLOW **1.5 hours**

START **Piazza Venezia**

FINISH **Piazza Barberini Metro**

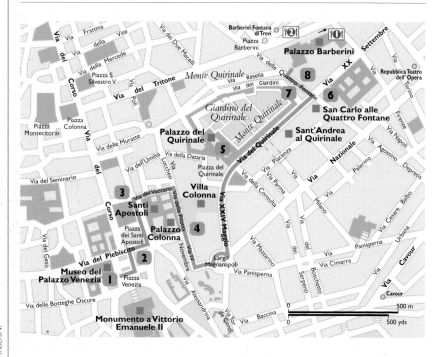

gardens across the street. Palazzo Colonna is built over an ancient Serapeum, a temple to the Egyptian god, Serapis, which was later surmounted by a castle. The castle belonged to the Colonna family – one of the few aristocratic lines to survive the plots and perils of medieval Roman politics. The interior rooms are decorated with lavish frescos and the gallery consists largely of 16th- to 18th-century paintings.

PALAZZO COLONNA;
OPEN SAT ONLY 9-1

4 Follow Via IV November to Largo Magnanapoli. Turn left on Via XXIV Maggio to Piazza del Quirinale.

Pope Gregory XIII built the Quirinal Palace as a summer residence for the popes to escape the malarial conditions of the Vatican in the 16th century. After Italian Unification in 1870 this palace became the official residence of the Savoia King. From 1947 onwards it has been the home of the President of the Republic. The *corazzieri*, who guard the

building, are an elite branch of the carabinieri who are all well over six feet tall. The fountain in the square depicts Castor and Pollux, the twin sons of Jupiter and patron gods of horsemanship. These huge statues are ancient Roman copies of Greek statues from the 5th century BC.

5 Leave the piazza turning left down what is now Via del Quirinale.

Sant'Andrea al Quirinale is a small and elegant church designed by Bernini (1598-1680) for Cardinal Pamphilj, nephew of Pope Innocent X, in 1678. Its nickname is the Baroque Pearl because of its pink marble decorations. Bernini, great sculptor of the Baroque, served ten consecutive popes as artist and architect. He was extremely prolific and won people over with his eloquence. His son once found him wandering like a tourist in the hall of this church and when asked why, he replied: "My son, I feel a special satisfaction at the bottom of my heart for this one piece of architecture."

SANT' ANDREA AL QUIRINALE CHURCH; OPEN DAILY 8.30-12, 3.30-7

6 Turn left on Via delle Quattro Fontane.

At the intersection of Via delle Quattro Fontane you can admire the four fountains for which the road is named. They feature statues of two reclining river Gods, Tiber and Arno, and two goddesses, Diana and Juno. The fountains were designed by Domenico Fontana and Pietro da Cortona for Pope Sixtus V in the 16th century. He was the pope responsible for an ambitious series of urban planning projects that included the erection of obelisks at principal pilgrimage sites across the city. The small church of San Carlo alle Quattro Fontane was the first major commission for Francesco Borromini, who was asked to work on an extremely tight budget – the brotherhood of the Trinitarian order that he was working for was not a wealthy one. The materials may be simple brick and stucco, but Borromini's complex and ingenious design reveal why he is considered the greatest innovator of Baroque architecture. Unfortunately, Borromini was opposite in character to his great rival, Bernini. His brooding, cantankerous and unbalanced character put him into conflict with patrons and fellow artists alike. He ended his own life in a fit of deep depression.

WHERE TO EAT

🍴 RISTORANTE TULLIO,
Via di S. Nicola da Tolentino 26;
Tel: 06 4745560.
You can get an excellent steak at this elegant family-owned restaurant.

🍴 HOTEL BERNINI BRISTOL,
Piazza Barberini 23;
Tel: 06 488931.
Elegant hotel with a roof garden..

SAN CARLO ALLE QUATTRO FONTANE CHURCH; CLOSED SUN

7 Continue down Via delle Quattro Fontane to Palazzo Barberini, which is found at No. 13.

Pope Urban VIII Barberini was keen on Baroque architecture and hired Carlo Maderno to redesign this palace as a family residence. After Maderno's death, the job was completed by the collaborative efforts of Bernini and Borromini. The Italian government acquired the building as the Galleria Nazionale d'Arte Antica in 1949. While you are here, don't miss the chance to see Borromini's elegant spiral stairway in the right wing and Raphael's *La Fornarina* (1518–19).

PALAZZO BARBERINI; OPEN TUE-SUN
8.30-7.30 www.galleriaborghese.it

8 The walk ends here. You can take the metro from Piazza Barberini at the end of Via delle Quattro Fontane.

61

Divine Esquiline

Uncover the spectacular mosaics of the Byzantine era, inspired by divine light but hidden in the darkness of Rome's early Christian churches.

Today most of Rome's churches are in the grand style, with Baroque façades, intricate sculpture and colourful marble, but the exteriors of early Christian churches were unadorned. Inside these plain brick edifices, divinely inspired artists created shimmering Byzantine mosaics to reflect the glory of heaven, the beauty of the soul and the light of God. Gold leaf was applied to the back of many of the glass tiles used in these mosaics, so that in the flickering candlelight of Mass, God and the saints would seem to hover above the worshippers. In this way the early Christian church became a metaphor for the human being. Its plain exterior symbolized the body and the carnal world, while its glorious interior symbolized the internal beauty of the soul, visible only to God. The martyred saints who walk beside us on this tour understood this concept well. They sacrificed their bodies to ensure the eternal salvation of their souls.

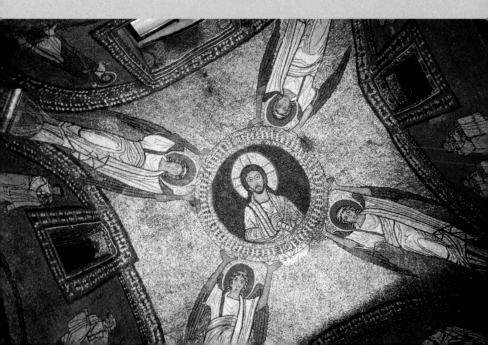

1 Take Metro Line B to Cavour and turn north out of the station down Via Urbana, which runs parallel to Via Cavour on the north side.

The entrance to Santa Pudenziana is on Via Urbana. Legend has it that this church is built on the site of a Roman house where St Peter lived for several years, converting its owner, Roman Senator Q. Cornelius Pudens, and his two daughters, Pudenziana and Prassede, to the Christian faith. Pudenziana and Prassede diligently buried the bones of martyrs. The church dates back to the time of Pope Pius I in AD 140 and its 4th-century apse mosaic is unique – notice how the apostles look like Roman senators. This is thought to be the earliest surviving Christian mosaic in Rome.

2 Turn right on Via Agostino Depretis to Piazza Esquilino.

The Seven Hills of Rome are the Palatine, Capitoline, Viminal, Quirinal, Celian, Aventine and the Esquiline, which now lies below your feet. The hill rises to a plateau of 207ft (63m), but its gradual incline is less noticeable than it would have been in ancient times. During Nero's reign, this whole area formed part of his 200 acre (81ha) park. In the Middle Ages it was littered with the watchtowers of Roman residences. Today it is home to the church of Santa Maria Maggiore.

3 Head right down Via Liberiana and cross Via dell'Olmata to Piazza Santa Maria Maggiore.

Santa Maria Maggiore, dedicated to the Virgin Mary, was built in the 5th century over the site of an ancient temple dedicated to Juno Lucina, mother goddess. Obviously it seemed like the right spot. The outside of the church was redesigned in the Baroque style, but the interior retains its spectacular original 5th-century mosaics along the nave. The church's special relic is the remnants of the manger that baby Jesus lay in. Legend has it that the ceiling is decorated with the first gold that Christopher Columbus brought back from America. At 246ft (75m) the church bell tower is the tallest in Rome.

4 Turn left down Via Santa Prassede. The church is on your right.

Santa Prassede church existed as early as the 5th century, but its current

DISTANCE 1.5 miles (2.4km)

ALLOW 2 hours

START Cavour Metro

FINISH Termini station

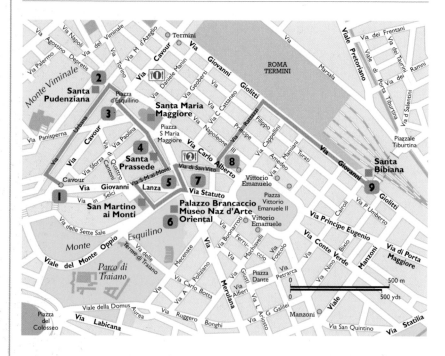

appearance dates to 822 when Pope
Paschal I rebuilt it as a place to house
bones and other relics taken from the
catacombs. It may have been built over
the home of St Prassede, who helped
hunted Christians hide from their
persecutors. Twenty-three of these
unlucky victims were found and executed
in her presence. On a column in the nave
sits a portrait bust of Bishop G. B.
Santoni. This is one of Bernini's earliest
works, done when the artist was just 19.
Santa Prassede's Chapel of Zeno is the

finest and most beautiful Byzantine
mosaic in Rome. Medieval Romans
called it 'the garden of Paradise' and you
will understand why as you walk into its
golden embrace. Pope Paschal had this
chapel built in honour of his mother,
Theodora. You can find her image here
– look for the lady with a square halo.
This indicates that she was still living at
the time of the chapel's decoration. A
jasper column in the chapel is said to be a
fragment of the one to which Christ was
bound before his crucifixion.

WHERE TO EAT

🍴 MONTE CARUSO
CICILARDONE,
Via Farini 12; Tel: 06483549.
An elegant restaurant with good wine
and excellent fresh pasta.

🍴 TRATTORIA MONTI,
Via di San Vito 13;
Tel: 064466573.
Sit out of the crowds in a family-run
relaxed atmosphere.

5 Turn right on Via di San Martino ai
Monti and left at the piazza on Via
Equizia.

Founded in the 4th century, the church
of San Martino ai Monti was originally
ascribed to Equitus. It was converted into
a basilica by Pope Symmachus (AD
498–514), then dedicated to St Martin of
Tours, the great missionary of the church
in Gaul. The church was rebuilt in the
9th century, but the Corinthian columns
decorating the nave are from the original
construction. The side aisles are decorated
with 17th-century frescos by Filippo
Gagliardi that document the appearance
of St Peter's and St John in the Lateran at
that time. The church now boasts more
modern designs by Pietro da Cortona,
dating from 1635-64. The façade dates
from this period and it was at this time, in
the 17th century, that remanants of the
ancient 'titulus Equitii' were discovered.
SAN MARTINO AI MONTI CHURCH;
OPEN DAILY 7.30-12, 4-7

6 Turn left on Viale del Monte Oppio
to the corner of Via Merulana. The
National Museum of Oriental Art is
found at No. 248.

The National Museum of Oriental Art is
a great place to stop if you want to see
something a little more multicultural and
off the beaten track while you are in
Rome. Pause here for a look at a superb
variety of art from eastern countries such
as Iran, Afghanistan, Tibet, Nepal, India,
Japan and China.
**NATIONAL MUSEUM OF ORIENTAL
ART; OPEN** TUE-FRI 9-2, SAT-SUN &
HOLS 9-7.30

7 Turn left on Via Merulana and right
on Via di San Vito.

The Arch of Gallienus faces Via Carlo
Alberto and is the last remnant of the
Esquiline Gates that marked the
beginning of the Via Labicana. It was
built by an equestrian citizen of Rome,
Marcus Aurelius Victor: the term
equestrian citizen meaning he was a man
of humble origins who rose to success
through his military service. He dedicated
its construction in AD 262 to the
emperor Gallienus and his wife. The
inscription praises him as 'a most clement
prince of unconquered virtue' –
Gallienus was leader during a time of
great crisis in the empire.

8 Turn briefly left on Via Carlo
Alberto then turn right on Via
Rattazzi and right again along Via
Giovanni Giolitti.

Via Giovanni Giolitti follows the length of Rome's main train station, Roma Termini. The station is named for the nearby Baths of Diocletian (the Latin word for baths is *thermae*) and is one of the largest train stations in Europe. The first Termini was built under Pope Pius IX in 1863, and the current building was inaugurated in 1950. The building's long curving shape has earned it the nickname of The Dinosaur. The church of Santa Bibiana can be found at No. 154. Bibiana was a young Christian martyr whose sister and mother were also martyred. St Bibiana is the patron saint of the Roman Catholic Archdiocese of Los Angeles. The church was originally built in the 5th century and restored in 1220 and once again during the Baroque period. In fact, its 1624 façade is a design by Bernini (1598-1680). The great Baroque sculptor's homage to Bibiana's sacrifice can be found inside the church to the right of the altar: it was his first effort at creating a religious non-nude.

9 The walk ends here. Turn right out of the church onto Via Giovanni Giolitti and head for Termini station, where you can take the bus or metro.

Scattered Remnants and Ruins

The contrast and conflict between ancient and modern Rome is a visible part of the urban landscape, especially along the road of the Imperial Fora.

The road leading from the Coliseum to Piazza Venezia is Via dei Fori Imperiali, the road of the Imperial Fora. By the time of Julius Caesar in the 1st century BC, the original Roman Forum was becoming far too crowded for the scores of new residents pouring in from across the expanding empire. Caesar, Augustus, Vespasian, Nerva and Trajan all built additions to the Forum to expand the town centre. Some of these areas remain unexcavated beneath the road. Rome's underbelly is occasionally revealed in the city's archaeological parks, but it often jumps out unexpectedly. Sometimes you can peer over rails at the roadside into an oasis of the old city's remains. Mussolini had Via dei Fori Imperiali made as a processional avenue from his headquarters in Palazzo Venezia to the Coliseum. The route opened up a view from his offices to the spectacular ancient monument – Mussolini often highlighted the past in his urban planning, and he wanted people to associate his leadership with the legacy of imperial Rome.

1 Take Metro Line B to Colosseo. Cross the street and turn right down Via dei Fori Imperiali.

Maps along the walls of the street document the expansion of the Roman Empire from a mere city in 509 BC to the height of Roman Imperial conquests under Emperor Trajan in the 2nd century.

2 Continue down Via dei Fori Imperiali.

The church of Santi Cosma and Damian was built under Pope Felice IV in 527 over the remains of a large library that was part of Vespasian's Forum of Peace. It is dedicated to two brothers who were doctors martyred in Syria in the reign of Diocletian (AD 254–312). Diocletian was the last emperor to try to exterminate what he saw as the unpatriotic cult of Christianity. The apse mosaic of the 6th century is splendid. Christ is depicted at its centre, surrounded by saints Peter, Paul, Cosma, Damian and Theodore. And of course Pope Felice IV makes an appearance as well.

3 Cross the intersection at Largo Ricci.

At the corner of Largo Ricci you get an excellent view of the excavated remains of the Forum of Nerva and the Forum of Augustus. The back wall that encompasses this area is made of volcanic pozzolana rock. It was erected by Augustus in an effort to shelter the Forum from the frequent fires in the Subura district

WHERE TO EAT

🍴 **RENATO E LUISA,**
Via dei Barbieri 25;
Tel: 06 6869660.
Good value back-street taverna near Largo Argentina.

🍴 **BAIRES,**
Corso del Rinascimento 1;
Tel: 06 6861293.
If you want to escape Italian cuisine for a night or just crave a steak, this is the place to go.

🍴 **ENOTECA CORSI,**
Via del Gesù 88;
Tel: 06 6790821.
No-frills trattoria and wine bar.

behind. These fires regularly swept through Rome – often the result of cooking on an open fire in the residential apartment blocks. On the same spot you can clearly see the base and columns of the Temple of Mars Ultor, Mars of Vengence. Augustus vowed to build this temple in honour of Mars if he was victorious over Caesar's assassins, Brutus and Cassius. In 42 BC at the Battle of Philippi, Caesar's heir finally had his revenge, but Mars had to wait 40 years for his temple.

4 Cross back to the other side of Via dei Fori Imperiali and continue.

You can see the original ancient Forum in the distance, but the remains that lie

DISTANCE 1 mile (1.6km)

ALLOW 1.5 hours

START **Colosseo Metro**

FINISH **Largo di Torre Argentina**

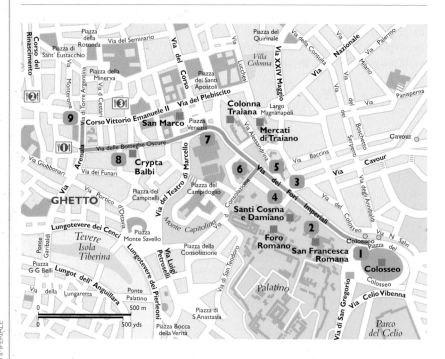

closer to the avenue are part of the Forum of Julius Caesar. Small columns and steps mark this area. Between Via Fori Imperiali and Via San Pietro in Carcere are the ruins of the Temple of Venus Genetrix. The temple was built to celebrate Julius Caesar and his family ancestry: the Julians claimed to be descendants of the goddess Venus. It was also a tactic to encourage the Roman people to have larger families as, by the end of the Republican era, wars abroad and a lower birthrate were seen as threats

to the power of Rome. Low birthrate soon became a major political issue in the city. Statues of the emperors once marked the centres of the fora, but now line up along the avenue. So to find out whose forum is whose, look at the statues.

5 Turn left on Via San Pietro in Carcere to the Mamertine Prison at Clivo Argentario 1.

The sinister Mamertine prison, known in Roman times as the Tullianum, was the

first ancient Roman gaol. Today it lies under the church of San Giuseppe dei Falegnami or St Joseph of Carpenters. It was originally a water cistern that was part of the Cloaca Maxima, or great drain of the Forum; prisoners who found themselves thrown into its depths had no hope of escape. Once inside, the Roman authorities generally left them to rot. Its most famous guests were Vercingetorix, who waited six years to be strangled, and

St Peter. If you are prepared to make a small donation you can descend into its damp depths.

PRISON MAMERTINO; CURRENTLY CLOSED FOR RENOVATION

6 Return to Via dei Fori Imperiali. Cross to the opposite side of the street and turn left.

The Trajan Markets were the largest and most spectacular addition to the original Forum. The coloured marble and rich ornamentation may be long gone, but you can still see that the markets were an impressive place. The architect was Apollodorus of Damascus, the most famous of the day and a favourite at the imperial court. At the far end towers the 65-ft column of Trajan, which was created instead of a triumphal arch to celebrate his conquests in Dacia (modern-day Romania). The relief sculptures depict the battles. Trajan's cremated remains were buried in its base and a gold statue of the emperor once stood on top. The statue perched there today is a figure of St Peter.

7 From Piazza Venezia turn left down Via delle Botteghe Oscure to the Balbi Crypts at No. 31.

The Balbi Crypts are part of the Museo Nazionale Romano or Roman National Museums. Here you can explore the archaeological discoveries of 1981 that revealed the Theatre of Lucio Cornelio Balbo, built in 13 BC. During the Middle Ages the theatre remains were used as

STATUE OF EMPEROR TRAJAN

tombs and artisan workshops. Visiting the museums is a great opportunity to see the underbelly of Rome, which mostly still lies buried in mystery.
BALBI CRYPTS; OPEN 9-7.45, CLOSED MON

8 Continue down Via delle Botteghe Oscure to Largo di Torre Argentina.

Today, Largo Argentina is the site of a real archaeological curiosity. Often overlooked, this square was excavated in Mussolini's time, when four ancient Republican temples from as early as the 4th century BC were discovered – some of the oldest in Rome. You can clearly see the ancient pavement, temple steps and foundations. Stretching westward beyond these temples, still lying hidden beneath the modern Roman pavement, was the Theatre of Pompey, named after the Roman Consul who had been Julius Caesar's principal rival for power just five years previously. It was here in 44 BC that a band of conspirators within the Roman Senate, among them Brutus and Cassius, stabbed Julius Caesar to death. It is said that the dying Caesar fell against the statue of Pompey and his blood poured over his feet... so Pompey had his posthumous revenge!

9 The walk ends here. Take any number of buses or the tram from Largo di Torre Argentina.

DISTANCE **1 mile (1.6km)**

ALLOW **2.5 hours**

START **Largo di Torre Argentina**

FINISH **Ponte Fabricio**

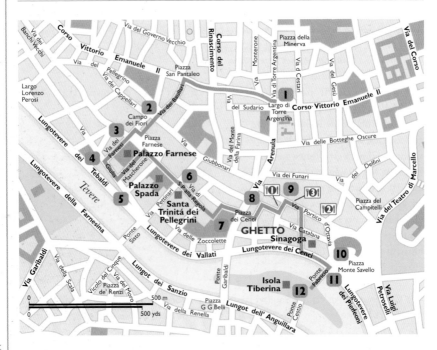

4 Turn left on Via Giulia.

Via Giulia is considered the most picturesque street in Rome. Named after Julius II, it is just over half a mile long and served as a principal route for pilgrims to St Peter's. It is lined with some of the most beautiful palazzi in the city. Architect Antonio da San Gallo lived at No. 66 and Napoleon's mother lived at Palazzo Falconieri, which stands beside Santa Maria dell'Orazione e Morte. At

Via del Mascherone is the fountain with the big mask that gives this street its name. In times of celebration it was made to flow with wine instead of water.

5 Pass under the arch and turn left down Via del Mascherone back to Piazza Farnese. Turn right on Via Capo di Ferro to Palazzo Spada at Piazza Capo di Ferro 13.

Palazzo Spada was first built in 1550 for Cardinal Capodiferro and its beautiful

stucco decoration is an example of Mannerism in Roman architecture, when artists defined their styles clearly and experimented with the strange. Cardinal Spada acquired it in 1632 and had it restored by Francesco Borromini. Today it holds his personal art collection – the only surviving small family collection in Rome, including works by Rubens, Dürer, Andrea del Sarto and Guido Reni.

PALAZZO SPADA; OPEN TUE-SAT, 9-1 SUN

On the following corner in Piazza della Trinità dei Pellegrini is the church of the same name, which means Sacred Trinity of the Pilgrims. In the 16th century it became part of the charitable association of Philippe Neri, founded to care for the many needy and ailing pilgrims travelling to and from the city. Inside is a poignant *Trinity* (1655) by Guido Reni.

CHURCH; OPEN SUN ONLY 11-1

6 Continue straight down what has become Via San Paolo.

Just past the church, on the right, is San Paolo alla Regola, where the perfectly preserved remains of a 2nd- to 3rd-century Roman house can be seen.

7 Turn left on Via Santa Maria Montincelli and take the first right down Via della Seggiola, crossing over Via Arenula to Piazza Cenci.

The palaces on the north and east sides of the piazza were part of stronghold created in this area by the Cenci family. This powerful Renaissance clan was one of several in charge of surveillance of the Jewish Ghetto. The family patriarch, Francesco Cenci, had a violent – and criminal – reputation among the Romans. His daughter, Beatrice, was known for her beauty and grace, but her stingy father locked her away to avoid paying a dowry. In the late 16th century his family hatched a plot to murder him. They beat him to death with hammers and threw his body into the river, but when his bloodstained sheets were pulled from the water the plot was revealed. To teach Rome's increasingly unscrupulous aristocrats a lesson, the Pope had Beatrice, her stepmother and her older brothers beheaded. Only the youngest member of the family, a ten-year-old boy, was spared.

8 Turn left down Via dell'Arco dei Cenci and immediately right on Via Calderari. Turn left on Piazza delle Cinque Scole (The Five Schools).

You are now in the heart of the former Jewish Ghetto. Jews chose to settle in this area, but under Pope Paul IV (1555-59) a wall was erected to enclose them. Jewish families were segregated behind the wall from sunset to sunrise and the main entrance was here on the Piazza of the Five (Talmud) Schools. Jewish Romans were finally given full citizenship in 1870 with Italian Unification, but the wall wasn't demolished until 1888. Mussolini's leadership brought tragic consequences to this community. Race Laws that restricted their rights were adopted in 1935. After the armistice between Italy and the Allies, Jews were targeted by the German occupiers.

9 Turn right down Via Portico d'Ottavia.

At No. 1 stands the house of Lorenzo Manilio, a Renaissance man deeply interested in ancient Roman history. Manilio chose to celebrate his family's lineage with an inscription and the use of Roman fragments in his 15th-century home. Via di Portico d'Ottavia is lined with charming restaurants and cafés. At the end of the street are the remains of temples dedicated to Jupiter and Juno built by Emperor Augustus in 23 BC for his sister Octavia. In the Middle Ages the church of Sant'Angelo was built on the remains of these ruins. Jews were forced to listen to missionary sermons here.

10 Turn right on Via di Sant'Angelo in Pescheria.

The temples became the backdrop for a busy fish market in the Middle Ages, as you can tell from the name of this road. The square on the corner of Via Sant'Angelo and Via Portico d'Ottavia is Largo October 16, 1943. The square commemorates the day that German occupiers surrounded the Jewish quarter and sent 2,091 Roman Jews to the infamous camps of Dachau, Auschwitz and Bergen-Belsen. Only 16 returned. The Great Synagogue rises to your right facing on to Lungotevere dei Cenci. Built between 1899-1904 by Osvaldo Armanni and Vincenzo Costa, its square dome distinguishes it from Christian churches.
SYNAGOGUE: OPEN DAILY, TIMES VARY
HEBREW MUSEUM: SUN-THU 10-5

11 At Piazza di Monte Savello, cross Ponte Fabricio to Isola Tiberina or Tiber Island.

The Ponte Fabricio is one of the city's oldest bridges, constructed in 62 BC. An inscription on its side dedicates it to a city administrator named Fabricio. Ancient builders added a prow to Tiber Island to make it the shape of a boat. According to legend, a ship full of conquering Romans was returning from Greece in 293 BC with loot from the temple of Aesculapius, god of medicine, when a sacred snake jumped ship. It was taken as a sign that the god's temple should be constructed on this site.

12 The walk ends here. Buses 23, 44, 63 and 280 depart north from Piazza di Monte Savello. Cross the river to take buses 23 or 280 south.

Scholars, Saints and Sinners

Nero's palace, a gladiator school and St Jerome's account of the first raid on the city – all found on one of the Seven Hills of Rome.

Like the Esquiline and Aventine the Caelian Hill was once crowded with the villas of wealthy Romans. It is now almost undetectable – the only remnant is the street of Via Claudia. In AD 64 a fire swept through the plebeian apartments and over the Caelian Hill. Emperor Nero took the opportunity to confiscate a large tract of land to build a palace complex that would come to be known as the Domus Aurea or Golden House. His eagerness to claim the land inspired the phrase 'Nero fiddled as Rome burned'. Nero spared himself no luxury in this 200-acre park and palace, built across the Palatine, Esquiline and Caelian hills. Eventually he was declared a public enemy and forced to commit suicide in AD 68. His lavish palace and its surroundings were buried by his successor, Vespasian, and forgotten for years. During the Renaissance, Raphael and his companions lowered themselves into the cave-like depths and, by candle-light, rediscovered the Roman wall paintings among the chambers of Nero's palace.

1 Take Metro Line B to Colosseo. Leave the station and turn left. Enter the Domus Aurea through pillars decorated with the face of Nero, which mark the beginning of Viale della Domus Aurea.

The Domus Aurea was so called because the entire front portico was covered in gold. Emperor Nero succeeded his stepfather Claudius at the age of 16 after his mother Agrippina poisoned her husband to make room for her son. But he was less than grateful and had her beaten to death. He then assassinated his wife, who was found with her limbs bound and her veins cut in a hot bath. He married his mistress, but kicked her to death while she was pregnant. Fortunately Nero was not able to enjoy his palaces for long before being forced out of power.

DOMUS AUREA; OPEN WED-MON 9-7.45, BOOKING IN ADVANCE RECOMMENDED

2 Leave the Domus Aurea through the gates and cross Via Labicana to Piazza del Colosseo.

The remains of the Ludus Magnus, Rome's main gladiator training school and barracks, are visible between Via Labicana and Via San Giovanni in Laterano. The school was probably three stories high with a central courtyard surrounded on all sides by small rectangular rooms for the gladiators. The complex was connected to the Coliseum by an underground tunnel. Although gladiators were trained professional

WHERE TO EAT

[O] HOTEL DEI GLADIATORI,
Via Labicana 125;
Tel: 06 77591380.
Rooftop garden with lunch menu, snacks, coffee, wine and cocktails. Lovely at sunset, or after dark when the monuments are lit.

[O] RISTORANTE PAPAGIO,
Via Capo d'Africa 26;
Tel: 06 7009800.
A historic culinary experience in which you can eat as the ancient Romans did.

fighters, they were generally regarded as slaves in ancient Rome. Some rose to celebrity, but most died in the service of entertainment.

3 Cross Piazza del Colosseo and turn left on Via Claudia.

Along the right side of Via Claudia are the remains of the Temple of Claudius, built by Emperor Claudius's second wife – and probable assassin – Agrippina, and dedicated to her hapless deceased husband in AD 54. Claudius, known as the accidental emperor, was born with a debilitating stutter and other physical imperfections. He suffered from bad health and had poor taste in women – his first wife, the malevolent Messalina, had a public wedding ceremony with her lover. As a result, Claudius had no choice but to have her killed.

OPPOSITE: DOMUS AUREA

DISTANCE 1 mile (1.6km)

ALLOW 1.5 hours

START **Colosseo Metro**

FINISH **Circo Massimo Metro**

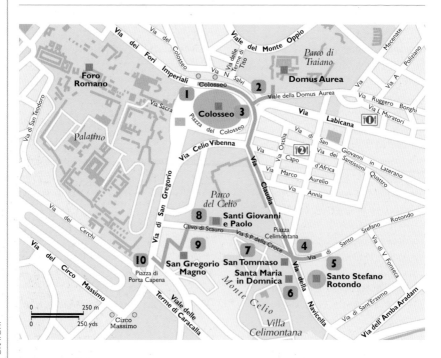

4 Turn left on Via di Santo Stefano Rotondo.

At No. 7 you will come to the round church of St Stephen, one of the oldest Italian churches built on a circular plan. The interior columns were recycled from ancient temples and buildings when Pope Simplicius commissioned the church in the 5th century. In one of the chapels you can see a carved marble seat said to be the throne of sainted Pope Gregory the Great from about AD 580. This pope was

known as a brilliant administrator and diplomat, but he was also a wise spiritual leader. He disapproved of the trade in relics, calling it distasteful and absurd, perhaps because he had witnessed Greek monks digging for martyrs' bones in a pagan cemetery.

5 Return to Via della Navicella and turn left to Piazza della Navicella.

Piazza della Navicella is named for the 16th-century fountain at its centre, which

is in the shape of a boat. The fountain is a copy of an antique one, made at the request of Pope Leo X of the Medici family. The church of Santa Maria in Domnica was founded in the 9th century and in its beautiful Byzantine apse mosaic you can spot Pope Pascal I kneeling at the feet of the Virgin Mary.

6 Turn left back down Via della Navicella to Via San Paolo della Croce.

To walk down Via San Paolo della Croce, you must pass under the Arch of Dolabella. Standing beside the somewhat abandoned church of San Tommaso in Formis, the arch was named after Cornelius Dolabella, who had it built in AD 10 on the site of the original Servian Walls of Rome. These city fortifications were constructed after the Gallic invasions and the burning of the city in 387 BC. The Arch of Dolabella later became part of the Aqua Marcia, an extension of Claudius's aqueduct that fed water to the Imperial Palaces of the Palatine Hill. Stretching off to the left, behind the church of San Tommaso, is the Villa Celimontana. This was once the site of the Mattei family villa. One of the most powerful aristocratic families of the

SANTA STEFANO ROTONDO

Renaissance period, the Matteis controlled the reins of the church and owned five palazzi in Rome. Today the villa is the headquarters of the National Geographic Acadamy and is surrounded by a public park.

7 Head towards the end of Via San Paolo della Croce to the church of Santi Giovanni e Paolo.

The basilica of saints John and Paul is built over 2nd- and 3rd-century Roman houses that were used for early Christian worship and the remains of the houses can still be seen. The church's construction in the 4th century was sponsored by a Roman Senator named Pammachius, who is thought to have been a friend of St Jerome. Both Jerome and the church witnessed the first Sack of Rome by Alaric the Visigoth in AD 410. This event would begin the long decline of Roman domination. St Jerome wrote: 'Words fail me… The city that took captive the whole world has itself been captured.' It seems that the church was damaged in the attack and rebuilt shortly after. The Romanesque bell tower or campanile of about 1150 rests upon the remains of the Temple of Claudius. Its beautiful Moorish ceramic coloured tiles are copies of the originals, which are preserved inside the church museum.

8 Continue straight down Clivo di Scauro to Piazza di San Gregorio.

Clivus Scauri, as it was known in ancient times, is actually an ancient road named after M. Emilio Scauro, a 1st-century Roman censor, a high-ranking magistrate responsible for supervising morality. At the end of the descent is St Gregory's church. Pope Gregory the Great founded a monastery on this site in AD 575. It was long abandoned after his death, but a church was later built here during the Middle Ages. Pope Gregory devoted his papacy to reviving religious scholarship and charitable works and he served dinner to twelve needy souls every evening. A myth recounts that on one occasion a thirteenth person arrived unexpectedly, but Pope Gregory nonetheless welcomed him in to sit and eat with the others. It was in fact an angel who had come from heaven to test Gregory's generosity and good will.

9 Turn left on Salita di San Gregorio to Piazza di Porta Capena.

Piazza di Porta Capena is the site of the ancient southern gate of the Servian city walls, dating to around 550 BC. They were the first walls of the city and were nearly 7 miles (11km) long, but during the next 900 years, Rome would outgrow them. None of the gate's remains are visible today. An obelisk from the holy city of Axum, stolen by Mussolini during the fascist occupation of Ethiopia, once stood here. The Italian government had the obelisk dismantled and returned it in 2003.

10 The walk ends here. Metro Line B is just a few feet away at Circo Massimo station.

Street Statues and Stones of Rome

Take the backstreets of the city to discover the mysterious statues and stonework that literally became the mouthpiece of Renaissance Rome.

During the Middle Ages, pagan Roman statuary was seen as evil and disgusting by the early Christians, so much of it was destroyed or simply discarded. At the time of the Renaissance, which means 'rebirth', the ancient Roman sculpture formerly thought of as 'rubbish' was indeed reborn, as pieces were re-evaluated and appreciated once more as art. Often, finds would be incorporated into new buildings or used as urban decor. Gradually, Renaissance Romans began to use the statues dotted around the city as 'spokespeople' for their grievances. They began to attach satirical rhymes, scathing political reports and write-ups detailing the scandals of the times to them. Statues used for this purpose came to be known as *statue parlante* or talking statues. Renaissance Romans weren't guaranteed freedom of expression but, in this way, they managed to think of creative ways to communicate. By hiding behind their stone friends, they were able to avoid reprisals, which could range from verbal abuse to murder, depending on the nature of their allegations or assertions.

1 Take bus 30, 44, 46, 63 or 716 to Piazza Venezia and walk up to the Piazza del Campidoglio and the Capitoline Museums.

Piazza del Campidoglio was designed by Michelangelo for Pope Paul III and stands on top of the Capitoline Hill (the word 'capital' derives from the hill's name). It was the site of the most important temple in ancient Rome dedicated to Jupiter, and of the first meeting of the Roman Senate in 509 BC. Today it is home to the Roman town hall and the Capitoline Museums. These exceptional museums contain the Capitoline *She-Wolf*, the *Dying Gaul* and a wide collection of Roman portrait busts. Unlike their Greek predecessors, Romans rendered true likenesses of themselves in stone. Nero, Hadrian, Cicero and Homer are just a few of the people you will meet inside. In the courtyard of the Palazzo Nuovo you will also come face to face with Marforio, the reclining river god, once one of Rome's famous talking statues.

PIAZZA DEL CAMPIDOGLIO;

OPEN 9-8 TUE-SUN

2 Descend the Cordonata stairs. Turn right on Via del Teatro di Marcello.

The Cordonata stairway was built to allow horses to climb up to the Campidoglio. Its shallow steps make it a bit more attractive to the tired tourist than the adjacent stairs leading to Santa Maria in Aracoeli. That steep flight was built in 1348 for pilgrims to climb on their knees in the Holy Year of 1350.

3 Cross the busy intersection to Piazza San Marco on the left.

In the corner of the piazza to the left of the church façade you will see the remains of another of Rome's talking statues. Named Madama Lucrezia, she was possibly created as a likeness of Empress Faustina, beloved wife of Antoninus Pius. Renaissance Romans renamed her after a local brothel owner who was similarly physically endowed! The church of San Marco in the complex of Palazzo Venezia is dedicated to St Mark the Evangelist, patron saint of Venice, in honour of Pope Mark, who founded the church in AD

DISTANCE **I mile (1.6km)**

ALLOW **1.5 hours**

START **Piazza Venezia**

FINISH **Largo Argentina**

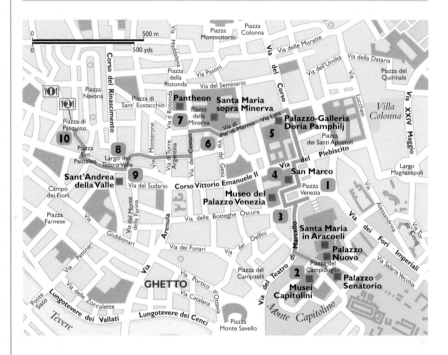

336 – it was the church of the Venetian community in Rome. The apse mosaic depicting Christ is 9th century, while the gilded ceiling and façade date to Renaissance renovations.

4 Leave San Marco and turn left and left again through Piazza Venezia. Head up Via del Corso to Via Lata and turn left.

Today the narrow Via Lata leads off of the Via del Corso, but Via Lata was in

fact the name of Via del Corso prior to the Renaissance. It was renamed in the 15th century for the carnival races, or *corse*, which took place on Rome's main streets. Even the pope would watch the entertainments. Various animals were made to race, and people dressed in elaborate costumes paraded through the streets. Just after turning left on Via Lata you will spy the Fontanella del Facchino. This fountain portrays a 16th-century water carrier and was yet another of Renaissance Rome's talking statues.

5 Walk through Piazza del Collegio Romano down Via di Pie' di Marmo.

The Collegio Romano, founded by Pope Gregory XIII, was the main centre of study for the Jesuits. It was taken over by the Italian government in 1870 and made into a state school. Opposite the Collegio Romano is the main entrance of the enormous Palazzo Doria Pamphilj. At the beginning of the 16th century this palace was occupied by Cardinal Fazio Santorio, but when Pope Julius II scolded him for the excesses of his grand residence, the Cardinal gave the palace to the pope's nephew, Duke of Urbino. Today the Palazzo Doria Pamphili is a museum of Renaissance and Baroque painting. As you pass through the piazza, stop at the corner of Via di Santo Stefano di Cacco to see the Piede di Marmo, or Marble Foot, that was placed here in the 16th century. It is a remnant of an ancient colossal Egyptian goddess – probably Isis or Serapis.

PALAZZO DORIA PAMPHILJ;
OPEN MON-SAT 10-5

6 Turn right on Via Santa Caterina da Siena to Piazza della Minerva.

Santa Maria Sopra Minerva (St Mary over Minerva) was so called because the church was built over an ancient temple to the goddess of Wisdom. This is the only gothic church in the city: notice the rosette windows and stained glass inside. The small statue of an elephant surmounted by an obelisk is by Bernini. Once it was finished, critics decided that the elephant looked more like a pig and so the statue came to be known as the Minerva Piggy. The Dominican priests who lived in the adjacent palace were constantly interfering in Bernini's project, so the artist took his revenge by facing the elephant's backside towards their windows. To the left of the church altar is a statue of Christ by Michelangelo.

SANTA MARIA SOPRA MINERVA;
OPEN MON-FRI 7-7, SAT 7-1, 3.30-7, SUN 8-7

7 Turn left on Via dei Cestari. Turn right on Via Arco di Ciambella. Cross Via di Torre Argentina to Via Sinibaldi. Cross Via Monterone and proceed down Via Redentoristi to Largo Teatro Valle.

SANTA MARIA SOPRA MINERVA

At the end of Via Redentoristi, look to the right for a beautiful view of Borromini's spire of Sant' Ivo alla Sapienza. These winding backstreets of the city are some of its most pleasant, being less crowded and therefore much more peaceful. In Largo Teatro Valle you have a good view of the church of Sant'Andrea della Valle (St Andrew of the Valley). In ancient times there was a small pond here where, according to Tacitus, Nero liked to sail. The Baroque church was begun in 1591 and is largely the work of Carlo Maderno and Carlo Rainaldi. Have you noticed that there is only one angel on the façade? When Pope Alexander VII complained that this angel appeared to be inelegantly stuck to the church, the offended artist told the pope to go ahead and sculpt the next angel himself. Giovanni Lanfranco is responsible for the beautiful interior frescos that depict the martyrdom of St Andrew. This apostle proclaimed that he was unworthy of crucifixion in the same manner as Christ, and consequently was crucified on an X.

8 Turn left across Corso Vittorio Emanuele to Piazza Vidoni to the left of Sant'Andrea della Valle.

In the corner of the piazza you will see another of the talking statues: Luigi Abate, a classical Roman figure wearing a toga. The pedestal on which he stands explains the process by which Romans used him to criticize or condemn the behaviour of powerful rulers and aristocrats while remaining anonymous.

WHERE TO EAT

🍽 NAVONA NOTTE,
Via del Teatro Pace 44;
Tel: 06 6869278.
Delicious authentic Roman pasta and pizza at a very fair price!

🍽 CUL DE SAC,
Piazza Pasquino 73;
Tel: 06 68801094.
Rome's oldest wine bar is popular with locals.

9 Go left up Corso Vittorio Emanuele. Cross through Piazza San Pantaleo and turn left down Via di San Pantaleo to Piazza Pasquino.

Brought here in 1501, the 3rd-century statue, possibly of Menelaus, king of Sparta, is the original and best-known *statua parlante* or 'talking statue'. It was named Pasquino after a local tailor, whose work inside the Vatican allowed him to hear the latest gossip and scandal, which he then made public on the statue using comedy and satire. It was first used for this purpose under the rule of Pope Alexander VI, whose sexual appetite and lavish celebrations were anything but subtle. Today, Pasquino continues to serve the same purpose, as you can see from the messages posted all over him.

10 The walk ends here. Return down Corso Vittorio Emanuele to Largo Argentina to take Tram 8 or buses H, 30, 40, 46, 62, 63 or 64.

Maestros and Old Masters

Discover the achievements of Rome's greatest Renaissance and Baroque artists and architects through the city's churches and museums.

Many consider Michelangelo to be the supreme artist of the Renaissance and Gianlorenzo Bernini his counterpart of the Baroque. The two masters had much in common. They were both sculptors by passion, but architects by requirement. They both survived into their late eighties and worked to the very last. Like all great artists they were highly self-critical, but their achievements above all others moulded the urban landscape of Rome. They became icons of art and creators of the city. Michelangelo inspired a generation of artists with his muscular figures. Bernini followed in his footsteps and perfected the theatrical presentation of expressive figures in motion. The walk starts on Via Nazionale, which stretches out over an area of Rome that was used for successful property speculation in the 19th century because it was still undeveloped at that point. The palaces and buildings are mostly modern. As the walk progresses through the city, you will experience modernism through the names of the streets and piazzas that refer to the Republic of Italy and its history.

1 | Take bus H, 40, 60, 64, 70, 117 or
170 up Via Nazionale to Palazzo
delle Esposizioni at 194.

Today, most people flock to the Via
Nazionale for its fabulous range of
shops. Also here is the beautiful museum
complex of Palazzo delle Esposizioni,
built between 1880 and 1882 by Pio
Piacentini for the Roman municipality,
making it truly a piece of modern Italy.
The façade is based on the theme of the
triumphal arch. Numerous temporary
exhibits, film festivals and modern art
shows are held throughout the year.

PALAZZO DELLE ESPOSIZIONI;
OPEN TUE–THU, SUN 10–8, FRI–SAT 10–10

2 | Walk up Via Nazionale to Via
Firenze and turn right at Piazza
Gigli to Teatro dell'Opera di Roma.

The Costanzi Theatre, more commonly
known as the Teatro dell'Opera di Roma,
has the distinction of being Rome's
principal opera house. The architect of
the neo-Renaissance building was Achille
Sfondrini, who built the structure in
two years; it was inaugurated in 1880.
If you are lucky enough to attend a
performance, don't forget to look up at
the largest crystal chandelier in the world,
hanging from the ceiling of the hall. It is
20ft (6m) across and weighs more than
6,600lb (3,000kg). During the summer,
the opera company holds outdoor
productions in the Baths of Caracalla.

PROGRAMME AT www.operaroma.it;
BUY TICKETS ONLINE AT www.helloticket.it

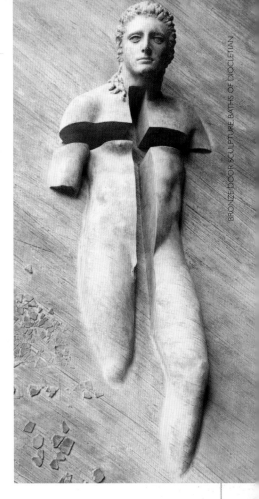

BRONZE DOOR SCULPTURE BATHS OF DIOCLETIAN

3 | Turn left on Via del Viminale to
Palazzo Massimo museum at Largo
Villa Peretti 1.

Palazzo Massimo is part of the National
Roman Museum and is well known
for its collection of ancient statuary
and Roman mosaics. The museum was
inaugurated in 1889 in a palace once
belonging to Pope Sixtus V. The vast
museum collection continues across

OPPOSITE: PALAZZO MASSIMO

DISTANCE **1.5 miles (2.4km)**

ALLOW **2 hours**

START **Via Nazionale**

FINISH **Porta Pia**

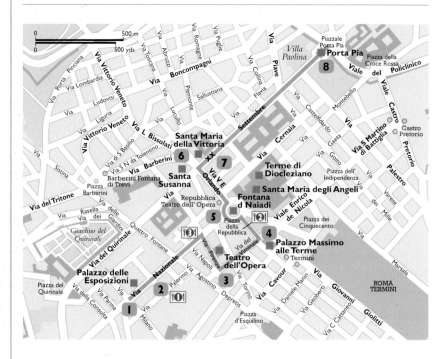

Piazza della Repubblica in the ruins of the Baths of Diocletian. These most sumptuous of all the imperial bath complexes continued to be used until the Goth invaders destroyed the aqueducts in AD 537.

PALAZZO MASSIMO; OPEN TUE-SUN 9-7.

4 Turn left on Via di Terme di Diocleziano to Piazza Repubblica.

The traffic roundabout in Piazza Repubblica is centred on an elaborate

fountain designed in 1888 and called Fountain of the Naiads, after the mythical virgin nymphs who preside over fountains and springs. The piazza's porticoed palaces date to the end of the 19th century. The church of St Mary of the Angels and Martyrs faces onto the piazza. Built over the Baths of Diocletian, it was designed by Michelangelo for Pope Pius IV in 1562. At a time when most architects were demolishing old buildings, Michelangelo used the old bath complex to create a uniquely shaped central nave.

5 Cross Piazza della Repubblica. Take Via Orlando to Piazza San Bernardo.

The church of Santa Susanna is the original source of the commonly repeated Baroque façade, designed by Carlo Maderno in 1603. This is the American Catholic church of Rome and Mass is conducted in English here. Across the piazza you can see the Fountain of Moses, built in the 16th century by Domenica Fontana to celebrate the repair of the Alessandrino aqueduct, which was promptly renamed the Aqua Felice in honour of Pope Sixtus V, whose name was Felice Peretti.

6 Leave the church and turn left, heading northward on Via XX Settembre.

The name of this road commemorates the assumption of Rome into the new Italian Republic. Santa Maria della Vittoria at No. 17 is the home of Bernini's famous masterpiece, *The Ecstasy of St Teresa* (1646). It can be admired in the Cornaro Chapel. This sensual and emotive work depicts Teresa being visited by an angel. According to the saint's account, she 'saw in his hand a long spear of gold and at the iron's point there seemed to be a little fire.' Not surprisingly, many modern scholars have interpreted this account by a Carmelite nun as a thinly veiled description of the orgasmic experience.

7 Walk down Via XX Settembre to Porta Pia.

WHERE TO EAT

🍴 **EST! EST! EST!**
Via Genova 32;
Tel: 06 4881107.
Pizzeria with pleasant staff and great *calzoni* (stuffed pizza).

🍴 **HOTEL EXCEDRA,**
Piazza della Repubblica 47;
Tel: 06 489381.
Open summer only, this rooftop restaurant overlooks the busy Piazza della Repubblica so you can enjoy the hustle and bustle from above.

🍴 **RISTORANTE PIZZERIA ZEUS,**
Via Nazionale 251A;
Tel: 06 48905444.
Wide menu selection, good fish and plenty of atmosphere.

The Porta Pia was renamed after Pius IV when he had this gate in the Aurelian Walls rebuilt by Michelangelo. The project began in 1561 and was finished four years later, but Michelangelo died in Rome before its completion, on 18 February 1564. His body lies with other great Florentines in Santa Croce in the city of Florence. In ancient times, Porta Pia was called the Porta Nomentana, after the northeasterly route it guarded to the town of Nomentum 14 miles away.

8 The walk ends here. You can take bus 60, 61, 62, or 84 back to Piazza della Repubblica.

Clandestine Cavour

Via Cavour is at the heart of Rome, but its treasures are often overlooked between the bustle of the train station and the ruins of the ancient city.

Via Cavour runs through the middle of Rome's Monti district. Rome is currently divided into 22 districts or *rioni*, according to a classification of the city that was established in 1921. Each district is distinguished by a coat of arms, assigned in 1744, and these are still visible today. The *rioni* derive from the original 14 districts into which Emperor Augustus divided the ancient city. Over the centuries, the number and borders of the districts have changed according to urban expansion and political allegiance. In antiquity this area was occupied by the Suburra, the crowded plebeian quarter. When Via Cavour and Via Nazionale were created in the 19th century, their construction completely modified the face of this *rione*. Modern Via Cavour is named after Count Cavour, the force and brainpower behind Italian unification. Via Nazionale and the adjacent road names indicate the modern roots of their construction under the new Italian Republic. The highlight of the area is undoubtedly Michelangelo's *Moses*, hidden away in the hard-to-find San Pietro in Vincoli.

1 Take Metro Line A to Vittorio Emanuele.

This square is named after the first King of united Italy, Victor Emanuel II. He was a member of the Savoy family, whose time in power was brief. The Italian royal family's support of Mussolini led them to exile in Switzerland after World War II until 2002, when they were finally permitted to reapply for Italian passports. Today the piazza is a busy market and one of the multicultural hot spots of the city.

2 Turn left on Via Leopardi to Largo Leopardi and the Auditorium of Mecenate.

The Auditorium of Mecenate was uncovered in 1874. A complex of porticoes, underground pipes, mosaic floor decoration and wall painting suggests that this is another Roman villa dating to the late 1st century BC. It is thought to have belonged to Mecenate, who was Minister of the Arts under Emperor Augustus.

AUDITORIUM; OPEN 9-1.30 TUE-SUN

3 Continue down Via Mecenate and turn right on Via delle Terme di Traiano.

Trajan's Baths were built here starting in AD 104 over the site of Nero's *Domus Aurea*. Today, this area is known as Trajan's Park. The impressive remains of the vast bathing complex can still be seen – the massive cistern, known as the *Sette Sale*, once held eight million litres of water.

4 Turn left on Viale del Monte Oppio, which becomes Via Eudosiana and leads to Piazza di San Pietro in Vincoli.

The church of San Pietro in Vincoli was built during the 5th century to house relics of the chains that once bound St Peter when he was imprisoned in Jerusalem. They can still be seen under the altar. At the back, to the right of the church, is Michelangelo's famous *Moses*. This statue is actually part of the funerary monument of Pope Julius II, the project that lured Michelangelo to Rome shortly before he was commissioned to create the Sistine Chapel ceiling. Michelangelo called this funerary monument the bane of his existence, because after the pope's death in 1513 his family members decided that they no longer wanted to pay for the original lavish and expensive

DISTANCE 1.2 miles (2km)

ALLOW 1.5 hours

START Vittorio Emanuele Metro

FINISH Via Nazionale

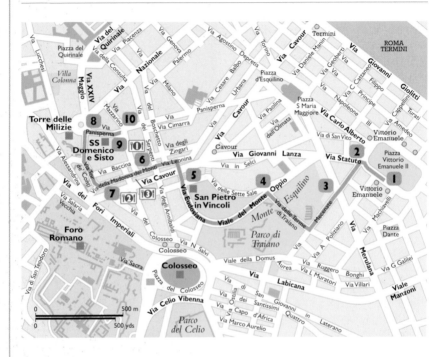

monument. The project kept shrinking with every year that passed. *Moses* is the principal piece and seems a fitting ode to a pope known for his courage, determination and authoritative manner. He is depicted with horns because of a mistranslation of the Bible.

5 Turn right out of the church, down the steps and head straight across Via Cavour to the parallel street of Via Leonina, which becomes Via Madonna dei Monti. Turn left on this road.

Santa Maria dei Monti's lovely façade was designed by Giacomo della Porta in 1580 as a miniature likeness of Il Gesù. The church is named after the Monti district and is one of the 28 titular churches discovered in Rome.

6 Continue down Via della Madonna dei Monti to Via Tor dei Conti.

To your left you can see the medieval tower that was once the tallest in Rome. Only the base is visible today, but it once

WHERE TO EAT

[◉] **AL VINO AL VINO,**
Via dei Serpenti 19;
Tel: 06 485803.
Wine bar specializing in a wide
selection of cheeses and offering
more than 600 wines.

[◉] **CAVOUR 313,**
Via Cavour 313;
Tel: 06 6785496.
Huge selection of wines with typical
wine bar food.

[◉] **ALLE CARRETTE,**
Via della Madonna dei Monti 95;
Tel: 06 6792770.
A handy pizzeria at the bottom of
Via Cavour.

stood between 165 and 200ft (50-60m)
high. It was the fortification tower of
the powerful medieval Conti family
and came crashing down during the
earthquakes of 1348, 1630 and 1644.

7 Turn right on Via Tor dei Conti. Pass
through Piazza Grillo until you
come to Largo Magnanapoli.

At the end of the road is the Torre delle
Milizie. This was another of Rome's
medieval fortress towers. It still stands
over 165ft (50m) high, but its upper
storeys were largely destroyed by the
1348 earthquake. At the end of the 13th
century it was owned by the Annibaldi
family, but it was later lost to the

expanding fortunes of the rival Conti
family. An erroneous medieval legend
recounted that it was in this tower that
Nero watched Rome burn… only about
1,200 years off!

8 Turn right on Via Panisperna to the
church of Santi Domenico e Sisto.

The church of Santi Domenico e Sisto,
dedicated to the saints Dominic and
Sixtus, is run by a Dominican order
of nuns. The upper external statues,
by Marcantonio Canini, show these
two saints. The lower statues, by Carlo
Maderno, depict St Thomas Aquinas and
St Peter of Verona.
SANTI DOMENICO E SISTO;
OPEN ONLY ON REQUEST

9 Continue down Via Panisperna to
the corner of Via Mazzarino and the
church of Sant'Agata dei Goti.

Sant'Agata dei Goti, or Agatha of the
Goths, was built for the Goths in AD 460
and then reconsecrated in 593 by Pope
Gregory the Great. Its current appearance
is 17th century. On the 18th-century
façade, facing via Mazzario, just above
the door, look for the relief showing St
Agatha holding her severed breast on a
plate: she was tortured when she refused
to renounce her faith in Christ.
SANT' AGATA DEI GOTI;
LIMITED DAILY OPENING

10 The walk ends here. Take buses
H, 40, 60, 64, 70, 117, 170 from
Via Nazionale or walk to Piazza Venezia.

Luxury and
Bare Bones

A walk evoking both glamour and horror as you head up high-class Via Veneto, home to a gruesome crypt and the riches of the Borghese gallery.

The famous crypt of the Capuchin monks, decorated with human bones, has captured the curiosity of many of Rome's visitors. The chambers are covered in elaborate designs made entirely from monks' kneecaps, ribs and skulls. From there you will walk up Via Veneto, actually named Vittorio Veneto, or Veneto Victory, for the World War I Italian victory over the Austrians in 1918. It was known as the hippest street in Rome during the 1950s and featured in Federico Fellini's *La Dolce Vita*. It is twinned with Fifth Avenue in New York City – you will see why as you walk past its elite cafés and hotels. At the top of Via Veneto, hidden in the Villa Borghese, is one of the most important collections of art in the world. Treasures amassed by wealthy Cardinal Scipio Borghese have been on view in the museum since 1903, including masterpieces by the greatest – Raphael, Bernini, Caravaggio, Titian and Canova. Once you have experienced the wealth of this collection you will find it hard to believe that at one time it was even larger. Many of its treasures are now housed in the Louvre in Paris.

| Take Metro Line A to Barberini Fontana Trevi station.

Piazza Barberini, named for the aristocratic Florentine family that lived in the area, is marked by Bernini's graceful *Fountain of the Triton* (1642), executed for Pope Urban VIII Barberini. Mythical sea creatures were a popular theme during the Baroque era. The piazza was once used to display unknown corpses for identification – often unfortunate pilgrims who fell victim to the plague.

2 Head north up Via Veneto to the church of Santa Maria della Concezione at No. 27.

On the corner of Via Veneto is a simpler fountain by Bernini of a seashell decorated with three bumblebees, symbol of the Barberini family. Its inscription invites thirsty passers-by to drink – go ahead! Santa Maria della Concezione stands just past this fountain on the right of Via Veneto. It is better known to tourists as the Capuchin bone church. The crypt is decorated with the bones of the Capuchin monks who served the order. Almost 4,000 skeletons were used in this macabre, yet poignant, display of human mortality. The Latin inscription above the exit once read, 'That which you are, we once were. That which we are, you will become'. The plaque is now found inside the church.

CRYPT; OPEN FRI-WED 9-12, 1-6

3 Continue down Via Veneto.

The Hotel Majestic at No. 50, founded 1889, is the oldest hotel on the Via Veneto. Most of the furniture is original. Madonna and Sylvester Stallone number among its guests. Palazzo Margherita, at the corner of Via L. Bissolati, has been the seat of the US Embassy since 1931. It is named after Queen Margherita, who came to live here after the death of her husband, King Umberto I.

4 Pass through Largo Fellini and under the archway of Porta Pinciana.

Largo Fellini is named afetr Rome's most famous film maker who included this road in *La Dolce Vita*. The brick archway marking the end of Via Veneto is the Porta Pinciana. This entrance in the 3rd-century Aurelian Walls was constructed in AD 403 and was previously named after Belisarius, who built the cylindrical towers to defend Rome from the Goths. Only the central arch is original.

DISTANCE **1 mile (1.6km)**

ALLOW **1.5 hours**

START **Barberini Fontana Trevi Metro**

FINISH **Piazzale Brasile**

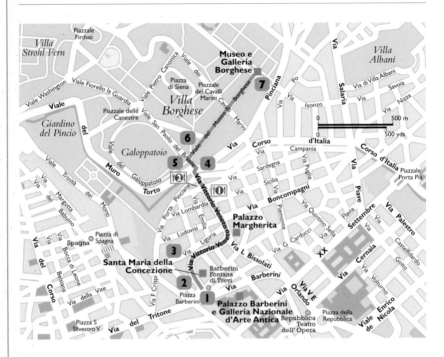

5 Cross through the busy traffic intersection of the Piazzale Brasile into the Villa Borghese.

The Propilei delle Aquile or Eagle Gateway, which marks the entrance to the Villa Borghese, was built by Antonio Asprucci in 1790. The eagles perched on high are symbols of the Borghese family. The Borghese acquired a small suburban vineyard here in 1580 and continued to enlarge and enrich the property with fountains, monuments, sculptures and gardens over following generations. It is commonly known as the Park of Museums and became the property of the Italian government in 1901.

6 Turn right down Viale del Museo Borghese and continue down to Galleria Borghese.

Entering the park, you will see on your left a handsome commemorative statue of Lord Byron by the Icelandic sculptor Bertel Thorvaldsen. The palace of the

WHERE TO EAT

🍽️ **GRAN CAFÉ DONEY,**
Via Vittorio Veneto 145;
Tel: 06 47082805.
Hotel lounge open for breakfast,
lunch and dinner, but best known
for cocktails and live music.

🍽️ **HARRY'S BAR,**
Via Vittorio Veneto 150;
Tel: 06 484643.
American piano bar and upmarket
restaurant serving lavishly presented
food and fine wines.

Villa Borghese was built between 1613
and 1616 by the Flemish architect Ivan
van Santen. It houses what remains of the
collection of Cardinal Scipio Borghese, a
nephew of Pope Paul V, who was known
as quite a hedonist. Given the current
richness of the collection, it is surprising
to know that much of it was in fact
sold to Napoleon by Prince Camillo
Borghese and now belongs to the Louvre.
It includes Bernini's *Apollo and Daphne*,
Titian's *Sacred and Profane Love*, Canova's
famous sculpture of Pauline Borghese,
Raphael's *Entombment of Christ* and an
extensive number of Caravaggios.
GALLERIA BORGHESE; OPEN TUE-SUN
8.30-7.30. BOOK IN ADVANCE
www.galleriaborghese.it

7 The walk ends here. You can take
bus 95, 116 or 119 from Piazzale
Brasile back down Via Veneto to Piazza
Barberini.

Stepping Up in Style

Walk up the famous Spanish Steps, explore the gardens of Villa Borghese on the Pincian Hill and visit some of Rome's best museums.

The Pincian Hill, well outside the ancient city centre, was never one of the Seven Hills of Rome. The Spanish Steps were an urban development project to unite it with the city below. Now they lead you across to the Villa Borghese. In the past, this villa was known as the *luogo delle delizie* or Place of Pleasures, because its vast gardens were filled with sculptures, fountains and country palaces. It was the suburban villa of the Borghese family and was covered in vineyards. The family bought it in 1580 and spent the next 100 years expanding and beautifying it. The huge park was organized into two formal gardens and a wild area. It was finally opened to the public at the end of the 18th century, when Marcantonio Borghese restored the villa and park, admitting visitors six days a week. On the other side of the hill are Rome's Gallery of Modern Art and a beautiful 16th-century papal villa housing a collection of Etruscan art.

1 Take Metro Line A to Spagna. Climb the Spanish Steps to Piazza Trinità dei Monti.

Trinità dei Monti church was founded for the French community by King Charles VIII of France and built between 1502 and 1587. Its name means the Trinity of the Hills as it is dedicated to the Trinity and sits atop the Pincian Hill. From here you have a good view of Piazza di Spagna and down the famous Via dei Condotti. The obelisk is an imperial copy of an Egyptian one and was erected here in 1789. Inside the church you can see several beautiful works of art, among them a painting by Daniele da Volterra, a follower of Michelangelo. His *Deposition from the Cross* (1541) shows Michelangelo's influence in the muscular forms of the male figures.

2 Turn left down Viale della Trinità dei Monti to the Villa Medici.

The villa is on the right at No.1. It was built in 1540 by Annibale Lippi for the powerful Cardinal Giovanni Ricci di Montepulciano, but it was purchased after his death by another cardinal, Federico de' Medici, and his name has been retained. Galileo was offered asylum from the Inquisition by the Medici Grand Dukes and stayed here under house arrest between 1630 and 1633 before recanting his scandalous belief that the earth revolved around the sun. The rich art collection that was once held here is now housed at the Ufizzi Gallery and Palazzo

Pitti in Florence. Napoleon took over the property in 1803 and from that time onward it has been the seat of the French Academy of Art. Across from the front door of the palazzo is a simple fountain with a cannon ball at its centre. Eccentric Queen Christina of Sweden shot it here – you can still see the dent in the door. **VILLA MEDICI;** OPEN OCCASIONALLY FOR CONCERTS OR EXHIBITIONS

3 Take the right fork on to Viale Mickievicz to Piazzale Napoleone I.

Along the avenue set back from Viale del Obelisco on the right is the Casina Valadier. Giuseppe Valadier, the landscape architect responsible for redesigning the Pincian Hill, created this small neo-classical building over the remains of a Roman water tank. It was opened in 1837 as a café, but only became a

DISTANCE 1.2 miles (2km)

ALLOW 2.5 hours

START Spagna Metro

FINISH Piazzale di Villa Giulia

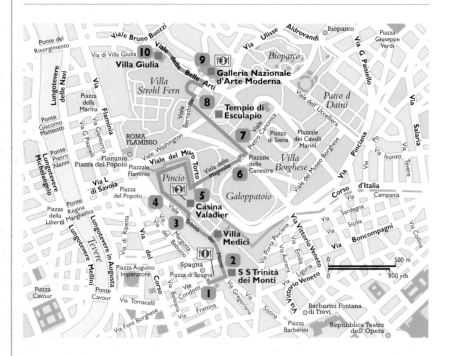

fashionable rendezvous during World War I. From Piazzale Napoleone I you can admire beautiful views of central Rome. You can also rent covered quadricycles on which to explore the park and surrounding areas.

4 Leave Piazzale Napoleone I and turn right down Viale Valadier, then right on Viale dell'Orologio.

Here you will discover the 16th-century water clock designed by a Dominican

priest named Embriaco. His name sounds very much like the Italian word for drunk. You will also see dozens of busts that decorate the paths in this section of the park. Giuseppe Mazzini, the eloquent voice of Italian Unification, had them placed here in the 19th century. They represent important Italian historical figures, but many have been vandalized over the years.

5 Turn left on Viale delle Magnolie, crossing the road bridge.

The Pincian Hill was connected to Villa Borghese in 1908 by an overpass, from which you can see the Viale del Muro Torto, meaning winding wall road. This highway follows the snaking Aurelian Walls. Viale delle Magnolie is named for its huge magnolia trees. Further along to the left you can cool off by dipping your feet in the huge round fountain.

6 Cross the intersection at Piazzale delle Canestre.

After crossing the intersection on your right, you will arrive at the only remaining pieces of the Aqua Felix aqueduct – stone reliefs depicting a lion and two griffins that were built into the wall in 1610.

7 Turn left onto Viale dell' Aranciera to the lake.

This path leads into the only English gardens to be found in Rome. At the centre of the artificial lake there is a small neo-classical temple devoted to Aesculapius, god of medicine. These gardens were part of the restoration project undertaken by Marcantonio Borghese in the 18th century.

8 Continue past the lake down Viale Madama Letizia. Turn right at Piazza Borghese and down the steps to Piazzale M. Cervantes to the Gallery of Modern Art at Viale delle Belle Arti 131.

At the bottom of the steps you can see the Gallery of Modern Art as it emerges over the crest of the hill. While most of us don't associate modern art with Rome, this collection of 19th- and 20th-century European art is truly a joy for the senses. Founded in 1883, it contains works by Antonio Canova, Gustav Klimt, Claude Monet and Vincent Van Gogh.

GALLERY OF MODERN ART;
OPEN TUE-SUN 8.30-7.30

9 Turn left down Viale delle Belle Arti to Villa Giulia at Piazzale di Villa Giulia 9.

This beautiful palazzo, built as a summer residence for Pope Julius III between 1550 and 1555 by the architect Vignola, was where Queen Christina of Sweden stayed in 1655 on her arrival in Rome. Today, you can enjoy the superb interior

WHERE TO EAT

🍴 BABINGTON'S TEA ROOMS,
Piazza di Spagna 23;
Tel: 06 6786027.
Founded in 1893 by two English ladies with a passion for tea.

🍴 CASINA VALADIER,
Villa Borghese, Piazza Bucarest;
Tel: 06 69922090.
www.casinavaladier.it
Elite dining for those who wish to spoil themselves.

🍴 RISTORANTE GALLERIA NAZIONALE D'ARTE MODERNA,
Viale delle Belle Arti 131;
Tel: 06 322981.
A restaurant located inside the museum.

frescoes and admire the design of the Renaissance palazzo as you meander through the impressive collection of Etruscan art, founded in 1889. The Etruscans dominated central Italy before Rome's rise to power and the art and culture they left behind had a major influence on Rome. This museum is dedicated to the preservation of this fascinating pre-Roman civilization.

VILLA GIULIA; OPEN TUE-SUN 8.30-7.30

10 The walk ends here. Tram 3 or 19 runs along Viale delle Belle Arti, but if you are heading back to the city centre it is much faster to walk down Via Flaminia to Metro Line A.

Skulduggery on the Docks

Stroll through the ancient harbour area where merchants traded goods newly arrived in Rome from all parts of the Mediterranean.

The area known as the *Forum Boarium,* or cattle market, was one of the oldest and most important marketplaces in the ancient city. It was the main city port during the 3rd and 2nd centuries BC, at the time when Rome was fast becoming a major Mediterranean power. Even today, it is easy to imagine the hustle and bustle of this commercial and social centre at the heart of the ancient metropolis. Naturally there is a temple to Portunus, the god of ports, here. The market fell into disuse after the construction of the port of Ostia under Trajan in the 2nd century, when this bigger and busier sea port replaced the older one. This area was frequently subject to floods and its marshy conditions were a perfect breeding ground for malaria. Today there is a concentration of temples, ruins and churches along the route. Highlights of the walk include a visit to the Mouth of Truth, perhaps the world's most famous drain cover, and the Roman amphitheatre Teatro di Marcello, the model for the Coliseum.

1 | Take bus 30, 44 or 95 to the church of Santa Maria in Cosmedin in Piazza Bocca della Verità.

This piazza is named the Mouth of Truth after the marble face that was originally a drain cover for the ancient sewer, Cloaca Maxima. In its second incarnation the face became a medieval lie detector. Suspected liars were forced to place their hand in the gaping mouth while someone wielding a sword hid behind it. The Mouth of Truth is mounted on the left side of the portico of Santa Maria in Cosmedin, on the corner of Via della Greca. Just a few years ago a car crashed into the church porch and the famous face was saved only by the strength of the portico columns. The church belonged to the Greek community and was built in the 6th century, then restored in the 12th. The bell tower was added during this Romanesque renovation. Its interior is famed for beautiful Cosmati floors and simple medieval decor.

2 | Cross the road after leaving the church.

On your left are two early temples. The round Temple of Hercules Victor was built at the end of the 2nd century BC by Marcus Octavius Herrenus, a member of the society of oil merchants who took Hercules as their patron god. The adjacent rectangular Temple of Portunus, god of ports, is almost entirely preserved. For many years its name was confused and it was known erroneously as the Temple of Fortuna Virilis.

3 | Cross back through Piazza Bocca della Verità down Via dei Cerchi and left on to Via di San Teodoro to Piazza Sant'Anastasia.

Sant'Anastasia stands between the Circus Maximus and the Palatine Hill that rises up behind. It was common practice for the early Christians to build places of worship over historically important pagan sites to symbolize the triumph of Christianity. The church of Sant'Anastasia was built over the site of the Lupercal, or Wolf's Grotto, associated with the legend of Romulus and Remus. The Lupercalia festival took place here every year. In this strange ritual a goat was sacrificed and its hide cut into strips – which young boys would then flick at passing ladies to ward off infertility! An early church was originally built here in the 4th century, but the one that stands before you today dates to a rebuilding of 1606.

DISTANCE **1 mile (1.6km)**

ALLOW **1.5 hours**

START **Piazza Bocca della Verità**

FINISH **Piazza Venezia**

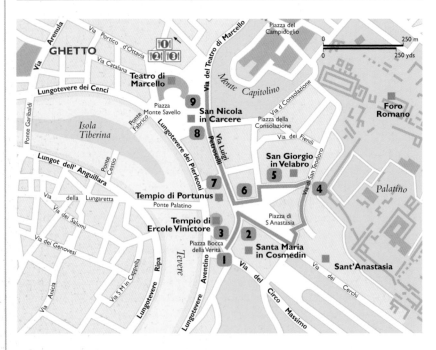

4 Turn left on Via del Velabro to San Giorgio in Velabro.

St George has been venerated as the patron saint of England since the time of Edward III, who founded the Knights of the Garter in 1348. George is believed to have been a 3rd-century soldier martyred in Jerusalem under Emperor Dacian. He was cruelly tortured and beheaded after refusing to assist in pagan sacrifice. It is probably around this act that the legend of St George and the dragon arose. However, it is more likely that the brave soldier rushed to save a goat, not a maiden. The charming little 9th-century church of St George in Velabro, or St George in the Marsh, is so named because it was built on what was once a flood plain of the Tiber. There is evidence of previous church construction and recent excavations have also brought to light some ancient grain warehouses. The Arch of the Argentarii (AD 204) or bankers' arch, still stands to the left of the portico. Rome's bankers and cattle

WHERE TO EAT

🍴 BARTARUGA,
Piazza Mattei 8;
Tel: 06 6892299.
This bar has an enchanting bohemian interior. Its name is an Italian joke – a pun on the word *tartaruga* or turtle – the bar is opposite the fountain on the piazza.

🍴 VINANDO OSTERIA-VINERIA,
Piazza Margana 23;
Tel: 06 69200741.
info@vinando.net
This small wine bar and restaurant in a hidden enclave has a quiet atmosphere, providing an oasis of calm at the heart of the city.

🍴 VECCHIA ROMA,
Piazza Campitelli 18;
Tel: 06 6864604.
Situated on a peaceful piazza, this restaurant serves good Roman cuisine and has tables outside for alfresco eating.

5 Pass to the right of the Arch of Janus back to Piazza Bocca della Verità.

The large square Arch of Ianus Quadrifons dates to the reign of Constantine in the 4th century. *Ianus* is the Latin word for passage and *quadrifons* refers to its four Roman arches. It was probably used as a covered meeting point in the busy market area. The keystone decorations above each arch show the goddesses Roma (goddess of the city), Juno (wife of Jupiter and patron goddess of young women), Minerva (goddess of wisdom) and Ceres (goddess of the earth).

6 Turn right on Via Lungi Petroselli, which becomes Via del Teatro di Marcello.

On Via Petroselli, at the corner of Via Ponte Rotto, is the House of the Crescenzi. This 11th-century house, built on the foundations of an ancient temple, and decorated with Roman relief fragments, was once topped by a medieval tower. The Crescenzi were Rome's most powerful family throughout much of the Middle Ages and often at the centre of corrupt papal affairs. However, their power began to wane after 998, when they headed a rebellion against Holy Roman Emperor Otto III. The family banished the pope, who had been selected by Otto III, and sold the papal tiara to a wealthy Greek. Otto III marched his armies to Castel Sant'Angelo and arrested the leader of the Crescenzi family. He ordered that his eyes be pulled

traders built it in honour of Emperor Septimius Severus and his family. Archaeologists have discovered that the emperor's successor and eldest son, Caracalla, later erased the names of his brother, wife and father-in-law from the monument after he had them executed. As you also saw in the ancient Forum on the Arch of Septimus Severus, Caracalla tried to erase all memory of his brother. Obviously, he was unsuccessful.

from his skull, his nose, tongue and ears removed, his limbs mutilated, his body dragged through the streets on the skin of a cow, and finally, his decapitation on the battlements. The corpse and its severed parts were then displayed on the gallows of Monte Mario with 12 other leaders of the revolt. After that, the family ceased to be quite so involved in politics.

7 Continue up Via Lungi Petroselli to San Nicola in Carcere at the corner of Via di Foro Olitorio.

Next to the cattle market in this area was the fruit and vegetable market – the Forum Olitorium. The small church of San Nicola in Carcere was built over the remains of three temples from the 3rd century BC. *Carcere*, meaning prison, refers to the former 8th-century gaol on the site. The church is named after the saint who is often identified with Santa Claus. St Nicholas is the patron saint of sailors, merchants, archers, children and students and had a reputation for secret gift-giving. The church was dedicated to St Nicholas by Rome's Greek community in the 11th century.

8 Continue down Via Lungi Petroselli to Teatro di Marcello.

The Theatre of Marcellus, a Roman amphitheatre, predates and provided the blueprint for the Coliseum. Julius Caesar began its construction and it was finished by Augustus in 13 BC. It held 20,000 spectators. Augustus dedicated it to his nephew and heir, Marcellus, who died

young. The Fabi family transformed the building into a fortress during the 12th century and it changed hands several times. The Savelli family rented its many arches to butchers and craftsmen during the 13th century. Today it is known as Palazzo Orsini because this family bought the complex in 1712. People still live in the top-floor flats. Beside the theatre you can see three columns and a segment of entablature belonging to the Temple of Apollo of 34 BC. Evidence shows that earlier temples to Apollo were built on the same site as far back as 433 BC.

9 The walk ends here. Take any bus from Piazza Venezia.

Romantic Rome

See central Rome through the eyes of the many poets and writers who came to the city to seek artistic inspiration and romance.

Before the arrival of the railways in the 1820s it was popular for young aristocrats, most notably the English, to travel through Europe on what was called the Grand Tour. Indeed, the Grand Tour became a rite of passage for many of the wealthiest young men in British society. Lasting from several months to several years, the Tour was intended to expose travellers to the culture and fashions of Europe, while broadening the mind. When in Rome, British aristocrats tended to favour the quarter of the city that surrounds the Spanish Steps – and it is from here that this walk departs. Nowadays, a cultural tour through Rome's streets and best-known sites is more affordable. This route follows in the footsteps of the Romantic-era Brits down the alleys of Rome to the great icons of the city, including the Trevi Fountain and the Pantheon. English influence is still evident in the names of various shops. For best effect, set off in the evening when the monuments are lit and a romantic mood settles over the city.

| Take Metro Line A to Spagna. The Keats-Shelley Memorial Museum is on Piazza di Spagna at No. 26.

Piazza di Spagna is shaped like two triangles meeting at the points. This quarter of the city is still marked by its British history – you need look no further than the Babbington Tea Rooms and the Keats–Shelley House. Babbington's was founded in 1893 by two elderly British ladies who missed a good cup of tea. The Romantic poets John Keats and Percy Bysshe Shelley lived in the house that is now the Keats–Shelley Memorial Museum.

KEATS-SHELLEY MUSEUM;
OPEN MON-SAT

2 Turn right through the piazza down Via del Babuino, left down Via Vittoria and left on Via Bocca di Leone.

On the corner of Via Bocca di Leone and Vicolo del Lupo stands the house where poets Robert Browning and Elizabeth Barrett Browning lived during their time in Rome. Elizabeth's father forbade this romantic match and the literary couple had to be married privately. Shortly after, they travelled secretly to Italy together where Elizabeth died in 1861. Her father never forgave Robert Browning.

3 Turn left on Via dei Condotti.

This is the most elegant and upmarket shopping street in the city. It is home to designer shops such as Gucci, Prada,

WHERE TO EAT

🍽 CAFÉ GRECO,
Via dei Condotti 86;
Tel: 06 6791700.
Oldest coffee house in the city; the favourite haunt of Casanova, Goethe, Keats, Byron and Tennyson.

🍽 ENOTECA ANTICA,
Via della Croce 76;
Tel: 06 6790896.
A reasonably priced wine bar serving hot and cold food.

🍽 ENOTECA SEVERINI,
Via Bocca del Leone 44/a;
Tel: 06 6786031.
Small authentic Roman wine bar.

Bulgari, Fendi, Louis Vuitton and more. The street's name is slightly less glamorous: Via dei Condotti refers to the water pipes that run beneath the street.

4 Arrive back at Piazza di Spagna.

The Spanish Steps, built 1723–25, were a late addition to the city. They were designed by architect Francesco de Sanctis to unite the Pincian Hill with the city below. In spring the steps are covered with flowers. During the hot summer months you can drink at the Barcaccia Fountain, which looks like it is sinking into the street – its name means 'bad boat'. Pietro Bernini, father of the famous Baroque sculptor, designed the

DISTANCE 1 mile (1.6km)

ALLOW 2 hours

START Spagna Metro

FINISH Pantheon

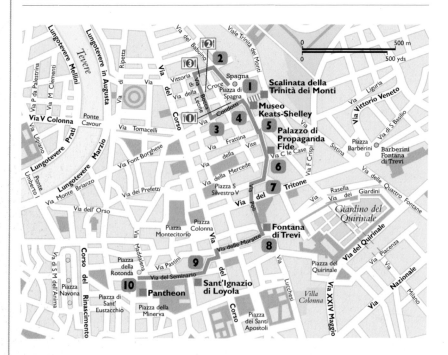

boat to commemorate the flood of 1598 and sunk it into the ground to resolve the problem of low water pressure.

5 Turn right. Walk past the Immaculate Conception Column and head right down Via Propaganda.

The column in Piazza Mignanelli commemorates the Doctrine of the Immaculate Conception, which was formally adopted by the church in 1854 under Pope Pius IX. You'll see a sculpture of the Virgin Mary at its summit. The pope hangs a wreath here every year. Facing the piazza and running along the left side of Via Propaganda stands the Palazzo Propaganda Fide. Gianlorenzo Bernini and Francesco Borromini both designed this palace as the seat of the Vatican missionary department to spread Catholicism to 'heathen and heretical lands'. Borromini created the elegant façade with intricate window frames, facing Via Propaganda. The personalities of these two brilliant Baroque artists

clashed on several occasions. History has judged Bernini a better sculptor, but Borromini the better architect.

6 Stop at the corner of Via della Mercede.

Around the right-hand corner of Via della Mercede, you'll find the often-overlooked portrait bust and inscription in honour of Bernini. This poetic ode to his talent says: 'G. Bernini, sovereign of art, who moved popes, princes and people to kneel before him, lived and died in this building.' On the opposite side of the intersection stands the church of Sant'Andrea delle Fratte. This was the Scottish national church until the 16th-century clash between King Henry VIII and the popes. Inside are Bernini's angels from Ponte Sant'Angelo. They were moved here from the bridge for safekeeping and replaced with copies.

7 Continue down Via di Sant' Andrea delle Fratte as it curves right. Turn left on Via Poli. Cross Via del Tritone and continue down Via Poli until you arrive at Piazza Fontana di Trevi.

The Trevi Fountain, the largest and most famous of Rome's fountains, celebrates the liquid of life and the source of fertility and health… water! Barbarian invaders in the Middle Ages paralyzed the city by destroying its aqueducts. The Trevi was created to celebrate the repair of the Aqua Vergine, an important aqueduct. The fountain took 30 years to build (1732-62) and was the life's work of artist

Nicola Salvi. Sadly, he died before its completion. Personifications of the four seasons stand atop its four columns and, at its centre, Neptune catches his balance on a seashell chariot skidding along the surface of the water. Notice how the wind ruffles his cloak.

8 Turn right on Via delle Muratte. Turn left on Via del Corso and right on to Via Montecatini to Piazza Sant'Ignazio.

This church is dedicated to St Ignatius of Loyola, who founded the Jesuit order in 1540. The saint's teachings maintain optimistically that we human beings can shape our own destinies. He advocated an active element to the priesthood in the sense that priests should be 'soldiers' of the church. This order was quite influential among artists, and most of the artists and architects who worked on the church were Jesuits. Orazio Grassi designed and executed the church architecture between 1626 and 50. Father Andrea Pozzo is considered the Baroque master of illusion. His spectacularly three-dimensional creations decorate the ceiling (1691-94) and most of the interior. Even the dome of this church is in fact only an illusion, or *trompe l'oeil*, by Father Pozzo.

9 Turn right on Via del Seminario to reach Piazza della Rotonda and the Pantheon.

The Pantheon is the best-preserved temple of the ancient world and an ode to the genius of Roman engineering. Dedicated to all the gods, it was

originally constructed between 27 and 25 BC by Augustus's right-hand man, Agrippa, to celebrate their victory over Mark Antony and Cleopatra at the Battle of Actium in 32 BC. It marked the beginning of Rome's peaceful Golden Age of Augustus. The original Pantheon was destroyed by fire in AD 80 and reconstructed under Emperor Hadrian in AD 125 to its original specifications. Even the inscription to Agrippa was restored. Walk through the massive original doors to see the largely original interior marble decoration. The dome of this building represents one of the greatest mysteries of Western architecture as no one can be sure how the Romans succeeded in its complex construction. It is a perfect concrete hemisphere, open to the sky through its oculus, or eye. The inevitable rain is drawn off through a series of drains in the floor. It was recently discovered that warm air rising from the crowded interior actually diverts rain from the oculus to keep the people below dry. In AD 609, Emperor Phocus gave the Pantheon to the church as a result of his concern for its conservation. Today the Pantheon has become the church of St Mary and all the Martyrs. Raphael's youthful corpse is entombed here, as are the remains of the first two kings of Italy.

PANTHEON; OPEN DAILY

10 The walk ends here. From the Pantheon you can walk down Via della Minerva straight to Largo di Torre Argentina where it is possible to catch a bus going in almost every direction: H, 30, 40, 46, 62, 63, 64, 70, 81, 87, 119, 271, 492 or 571.

Roman
Ramparts

Be amazed by ancient feats of engineering. Visit the Baths of Caracalla, an immense public leisure complex, then walk to the very edge of the city.

Heading south from the Circus Maximus leads you to the city walls and the beginning of the Via Appia, the southern route out of the city, and the road to Brindisi, the largest port serving Greece and the Orient. Today it is another of Rome's many archaeological parks and below it lie the tombs of some of the city's most elite citizens. The Baths of Caracalla are here: the best-preserved structure of their kind, they offer an amazing opportunity for visitors to experience the breathtaking scale of Roman construction. The massive brick walls would once have been covered in marble, and the halls and bathing areas were originally filled with elaborate sculpture. Even today, extensive areas of the rich mosaic floor are visible. When you reach the city walls that tower overhead, you will pass beneath the best-preserved of the city gates, Porta Sebastiano, which is another example of brilliant Roman engineering.

1 Take Metro Line B to Circo Massimo and turn right on Viale delle Terme di Caracalla; or take bus 118 or 628. Turn right on Viale Guido Baccelli up to Piazza Santa Balbina to the church of Santa Balbina at No. 8.

Santa Balbina was a young Christian martyr decapitated in the 2nd century. Her church was probably founded in the 6th century. It lies over the remains of a house reputed to have been her home, but was more probably the house of Lucio Fabio Cilone, Consul of Rome in AD 204. In the time of Pope Gregory the Great, this church was a fortified monastery. It went through many architectural transformations, but was restored to its original medieval appearance in 1920. The remains of a 1st-century mosaic can be seen in the floor.

CHURCH OF SANTA BALBINA; OPEN SUN 10.30-11.30AM

2 Leave the church and turn right down Via Antonina to the entrance of the Caracalla Baths.

The baths were named after Emperor Caracalla, first son of Emperor Septimius Severus. Septimius left the empire in the hands of both his sons, but Caracalla assassinated his younger brother Gaeta, then proceeded to erase his name from monuments and records. The Baths of Caracalla, finished in AD 217, the year of Caracalla's death, were expanded in the years that followed to cover an impressive 27 acres (11ha). Public baths were an important part of Roman daily life and included exercise areas, saunas, hot and cold reservoirs, and gardens too. The baths could accommodate 1,600 bathers and remained in use until 537, when invading Goths destroyed the supplying aqueduct.

CARACALLA BATHS; OPEN TUE-SUN 9AM TO AN HOUR BEFORE NIGHTFALL, 9-2 MON

DISTANCE **1 mile (1.6km)**

ALLOW **2 hours**

START **Circo Massimo Metro**

FINISH **Porta San Sebastiano**

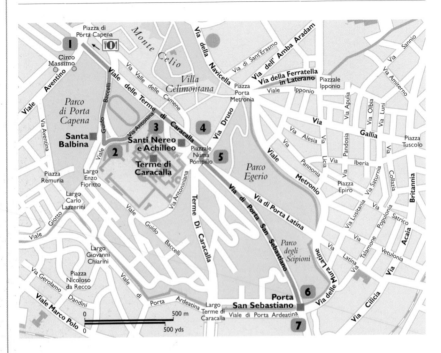

3 Turn right down Via delle Terme di Caracalla to Piazzale Numa Pompilio.

This piazza is named after the second king of Rome, who succeeded its founder, Romulus, and ruled between 717 and 673 BC. According to legend, this king was from the Sabine tribe and was a naturally gifted and wise leader who banished all trappings of luxury and lived a severe and ascetic life. In this he was quite unusual among Roman leaders.

4 Take Via di Porta San Sebastiano heading south.

At No. 28 stands the church of Santi Nereo e Achilleo. This 8th-century construction is dedicated to two brothers, converted by St Peter himself, who became martyrs when they were beheaded for their refusal to worship idols. The macabre frescos in the church, depicting their gruesome deaths, were painted in the 16th century by Niccolò Pomarancio. Nereo and Achilleo's

relics are kept here, along with those of their mistress, St Flavia Domitilla, who was supposedly converted by the two brothers. She was a member of the illustrious imperial Flavian family. The church is one of the tituli of Rome – early Christians had no houses of worship and used private homes for their meetings. Archaeologists have identified 28 such titular churches in Rome.

5 Head straight down Via di Porta San Sebastiano.

The Parco degli Scipioni extends along either side of Via di Porta San Sebastiano. This archaeological park marks the beginning of the ancient Via Appia Antica. It is named after Publius Cornelius Scipio (235-183 BC) who was the most famous military leader of the ancient Republic. He is even mentioned in the Italian national anthem. It was Scipio who defeated Hannibal and the Carthiginians in 202 BC to end the second Punic War. His family, the gens Cornelia, were buried in this area; however, he himself was buried near his villa in Naples. Before you reach the walls of the city you will pass under Arco di Druso (the Arch of Drusus). This arch is erroneously named after Drusus, a handsome soldier who was also Emperor Augustus's stepson. He lived between 38 and 15 BC, and died after a fall from his horse. But the arch is in fact a piece of the 3rd-century Antoniana Aqueduct, which fed the massive Baths of Caracalla.

WHERE TO EAT

🍴 ALVARO AL CIRCO MASSIMO, Via dei Cerchi 53; Tel: 0667861 12. Relaxed atmosphere with friendly staff and good food; booking essential.

6 Pass under the arch and through the Porta San Sebastiano, where the Museum of the Ramparts is housed in the gate towers at Via di Porta San Sebastiano 18.

This southern entrance to the city was originally named Porta Appia as it guarded the Appian Way. Porta San Sebastiano is the best preserved of Rome's impressive *porte* or city gates. Here you can get a true sense of the walls that once defended the seat of an empire. They stood 20ft (6m) high and 11½ft (3.5m) thick and boasted 18 gates – one gate just over every half mile (1km) or so of its 11 mile (18km) length – and 381 defence towers. Today the gate's towers are occupied by the Museo delle Mura, Museum of the Ramparts, that recounts the history of Rome through its impressive defences. Once inside, you can climb to the top for an excellent view of the Appia Antica.

MUSEO DELLE MURA; OPEN TUE-SUN 9-2

7 The walk ends here. Take the 118 bus back to Circo Massimo.

OVERLEAF: PIAZZA NAVONA

Escape to the Catacombs

Go beyond the city walls to the underground chambers of the early Christian catacombs, where saints and martyrs were laid to rest.

The Via Appia leads south from Rome. Today, as in ancient times, it is lined with funeral monuments and tombs to Rome's wealthy aristocrats. Under the pavement are the winding tunnels where early Christians buried their dead. It has been assumed that they must also have met and prayed here, but the presence of dead bodies would have created a rather unpleasant atmosphere. The origin of the word catacomb comes from the Greek *kata kumbas*, 'near the bottom of the valley', which indicates the original geographic location of these secret chambers. By AD 160 there were about 15,000 Christians in Rome, but Christianity remained illegal until AD 315. Early Christians had no places of worship and nowhere to bury their dead according to Christian ritual. Taking bodies to the catacombs avoided public persecution. Christian funerals were different from pagan ones: Christians interred the body for resurrection, while Romans cremated the dead until the 2nd century, when pagan Romans adopted the idea of burial from the Christians.

Take bus 118 or 218 to the fork of Via Appia Antica and Via Ardeatina.

The Via Appia Antica is the best-preserved ancient Roman road. It was built in 312 BC by the censor Appius Claudius Cieco and was the first road in Rome to be named after a person rather than its purpose (Via Salaria was the salt road, for example). After extensions in 190 BC the road went all the way to the port of Brindisi in the south. The funerary procession of Augustus moved south along this road to symbolize his passage into the underworld in AD 14. After St Peter escaped the Mamertine prison he fled along the Via Appia before supposedly meeting Christ, right here at the fork of Via Appia Antica and Via Ardeatina. The small church of Domine Quo Vadis commemorates Peter's meeting with Christ when the apostle asked, "Lord, where are you going?" and Christ replied, "I am going to be crucified anew."

2 Head right down Via Ardeatina to Via delle Sette Chiese and turn right to the entrance of the Catacombe di Domitilla at No. 282.

The catacombs of Santa Domitilla refer to Flavia Domitilla, wife of Titus Flavius Clemens, who lived in the 1st century, during the time of Emperor Domitian. Domitian tried to pass a decree ordering the execution of Jews and Christians. Domitilla's husband was Consul of Rome and under her influence he delayed its enforcement. According to Christian

WHERE TO EAT

🍴 L'ARCHEOLOGIA,
Via Appia Antica 139;
Tel: 06 7880494.
www.larcheologia.it
In this evocative restaurant an ancient tomb serves as the wine cellar. Traditional Roman cuisine.

🍴 L'ESCARGOT,
Via Appia Antica 46;
Tel: 06 5136791.
Cosy restaurant with a French twist.

🍴 RISTORANTE CECILIA METELLA,
Via Appia Antica 125;
Tel: 06 5136743. www.ceciliametella.it
Many weddings take place here and there's a large outdoor terrace.

legend it was Domitilla who arranged for the assassination of the emperor, so putting a stop to the decree altogether.

CATACOMBE DI DOMITILLA;
OPEN WED-MON 9-12, 2-5

3 Turn right down Via delle Sette Chiese to Via Appia Antica and turn left to the entrance of the Catacombe di San Callisto at Via Appia Antica 126.

Pope St Callixtus was a former slave and criminal in ancient Rome. He is said to have lost money from a Christian bank, fled Rome, got caught, and jumped ship to escape. He was also arrested for fighting in a synagogue. The catacombs of St Callixtus are famous for the Capella

DISTANCE **1 mile (1.6km)**

ALLOW **3 hours**

START **The fork of Via Appia Antica and Via Ardeatina**

FINISH **Via Appia Antica**

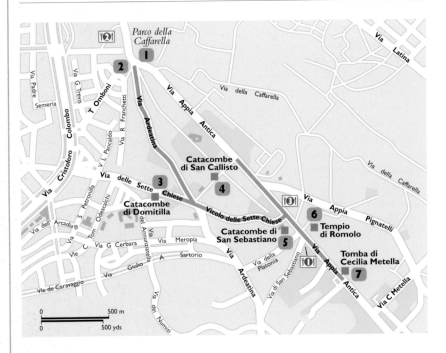

dei Papi, Chapel of the Popes, where nine popes of the 3rd century are interred. On 6 August, 254 assassins hired by Emperor Valerian are recorded to have attacked and murdered Pope Sixtus II in these catacombs while he was giving Mass. The 3rd century was a difficult time for Christians. The Roman Empire was in retreat across Europe and many emperors feared Christianity's growing power as a threat to traditional Roman ways.

CATACOMBE DI SAN CALLISTO;

OPEN TUE–MON 9–12, 2–5

4 Turn right (south) down Via Appia Antica to the Catacombe di San Sebastiano at No. 136.

These are the oldest catacombs in Rome. The church of San Sebastiano is a 17th-century building on the site of a basilica from the time of Constantine in the 4th century. St Sebastian was martyred in the 3rd century under Emperor Diocletian. Diocletian originally appointed Sebastian as an elite Praetorian Guard, unaware that he was a Christian. When he was

asked to worship Roman gods, as all government officials were required to do, his Christian faith was revealed. The emperor ordered him to be bound to a stake and shot with arrows. Miraculously, St Sebastian survived this ordeal, managed to escape and then returned to the city to proclaim the righteousness of his faith. At this point the authorities chopped off his head.

5 Proceed down Via Appia Antica.

On the left between Vicolo della Basilica and the tomb of Cecilia Metella are the ruins of a large 4th-century palace complex including the Tempio di Romolo (Temple of Romulus) and the Circus of Maxentius. These were built before Emperor Constantine's victory over Maxentius at the Battle of the Milvian Bridge. The temple to Romulus was dedicated to the son of Maxentius, who died young. The circus once held up to 10,000 spectators. Every circus had a platform called a *spina* at its centre, where decorative and commemorative monuments were raised – the obelisk of the Fountain of the Four Rivers in Piazza Navona once stood here.

6 Continue down Via Appia Antica to Tomba di Cecilia Metella.

This cylindrical mausoleum is the best-known tomb on the Via Appia Antica. It was ostensibly built in honour of Cecilia Metella, the daughter of a wealthy Roman Consul named Quintus Metellus

Cretius. This man was responsible for conquering the island of Crete in 69 BC. In fact, we can learn much about Cecilia Metella's father, husband and brothers from the inscriptions on her tomb, but we find out almost nothing about her! Her mysterious tomb and the strange obscurity that surrounds Cecilia provided inspiration for Lord Byron's

epic poem, *Childe Harold's Pilgrimage*. Her monument became the main tower of a Caetani family fortress in 1302 and you can still see the fortifications that were added to the top. The Caetani family rose to prominence in the 13th century after the election to the papacy of Benedetto Caetani as Pope Boniface VIII in 1294. The pope then began to systematically confer lands and noble titles on members of the Caetani clan, thus ensuring their rapid rise in status to the most notable family in Rome.

TOMB OF CECILIA METELLA; OPEN TUE-SUN 9AM TO AN HOUR BEFORE SUNSET

7 The walk ends here. Take bus 118 back to Circo Massimo.

Artists and Aristocrats

In the back streets and piazzas of central Rome, discover the art and architecture created by eccentric artists and their aristocratic patrons.

Ancient Romans built perfectly planned cities with perpendicular streets, but urban development during the Middle Ages transformed Rome's cityscape into a confusing jumble. Winding streets make the city centre a complicated labyrinth where it is easy to lose your way – it's tempting to stick to familiar and busy routes. But stepping just a block off the main road can make a real difference, often leading you to empty squares. Some of the most beautiful artwork and church interiors are under the noses of Rome's tourists, yet seldom visited. The city centre churches hold many masterpieces or are masterpieces themselves. This walk takes you through the Renaissance Florentine district once occupied by merchants and artists. You then walk an old pilgrimage route to see works by Raphael, Caravaggio, Bernini and Borromini, and see evidence of the eccentric and wealthy patrons who behaved scandalously behind the scenes.

Take bus 23, 40, 46, 98, 271 or 280 to Ponte Principe Amadeo Savoia Aosta or Piazza Paoli and make your way to Piazza dell'Oro between Corso Vittorio Emanuele and Lungotevere.

San Giovanni dei Fiorentini stands at Via Acciaioli 2 in Piazza dell'Oro. It was named St John of the Florentines after the community that it served and their patron saint, St John the Baptist. The church was commissioned by Medici Pope Leo X for his fellow Florentines and executed by the Florentine architect Jacopo Sansovino. Architect Francesco Borromini is entombed within the church. San Giovanni and San Lorenzo in Lucina are the only churches in Rome that actively welcome animals in the congregation.

2 Leave the church and head straight down Via del Consolato to Corso Vittorio, crossing through Largo Tassoni, and turn left on to Via del Banco Santo Spirito.

The Palazzo del Banco di Santo Spirito stands on the corner in Largo Tassoni. It was originally the seat of a bank founded by Pope Paul V Borghese in 1605, which has since been subsumed into the Banco di Roma. The north façade, built in 1520 by fellow-Florentine and friend of Michelangelo, Antonio da Sangallo, is modelled on a triumphal arch. On the side of the building you can see a lovely bronze plaque dedicated to Benvenuto Cellini who once lived here. This cranky sculptor was imprisoned several times on

WHERE TO EAT

|O| CAFÉ SANT'EUSTACHIO,
Piazza Sant'Eustachio 82;
Tel: 06 68802048.
Romans rave about the coffee! Watch the beans roast in the original oven.

|O| CAFÉ GIOLITTI,
Via Degli Uffici Del Viario 40;
Tel: 06 6991243.
Best gelateria in the city, in business since 1900. Order an immense, chocolate-covered cone topped with a melon-sized ball of ice cream!

|O| HOSTARIA DELL'ORSO,
Via dei Soldati 25c;
Tel: 06 68301192.
Rome's oldest tavern. Once the haunt of Clark Gable and Maria Callas.

charges of sodomy and died an old man in 1571, probably from syphilis.

3 Continue down Via del Banco Santo Spirito and turn right on Vicolo Curato, which becomes Via dei Coronari.

This straight road was built by Pope Sixtus IV of the aristocratic Florentine della Rovere family. It was the first straight street of the Renaissance and was known as the Via Recta, serving as a route for pilgrims to St Peter's. With all those pilgrims passing by, smart businessmen soon realized it was a good spot for rosary sales: *coronari* means rosary sellers in Italian. This lovely backstreet

OPPOSITE: SANTA MARIA DELLA PACE

22

DISTANCE **1.2 miles (2km)**

ALLOW **2.5 hours**

START **Ponte Principe Amadeo Savoia Aosta or Piazza Paoli**

FINISH **Via del Corso**

is lined with artisan shops. Look out for No. 122, where the artist Raphael lived. No. 156 was the house of Fiametta, the courtesan of Cesare Borgia. He was the illegitimate son of corrupt Pope Alexander VI Borgia and well known in Rome as a malevolent and dangerous character who literally, on occasion, got away with murder. He was even suspected of killing his own brother, who was fished from the Tiber.

4 Turn right on Vicolo del Arco della Pace.

Tucked away at No. 5 you will see the semi-circular portico of the church of Santa Maria della Pace. Like Via dei Coronari, this church was built by Pope Sixtus IV in about 1480 to celebrate the end of his war with Florence. The war came about because he wanted power over the Florentine Republic. He tried to undermine the Medici family and aligned himself instead with the rival Pazzis. Franceso de' Pazzi organized an assassination attempt on Giuliano and Lorenzo de Medici while they were attending Mass in 1478. Giuliano was slashed to death, but Lorenzo escaped to take his revenge. Franceso was stripped naked and hung from Palazzo della Signoria in Florence. Santa Maria della Pace houses some beautiful frescos by Raphael that depict the sibyls of Cuma, Persia, Phrygia and Tibur – pagan figures that feature in Christian art because they predicted the birth of Christ.

5 Leave the church and turn left to Via della Pace, then turn right. Turn left on Via di Torre Mellina, then left again on Via di Santa Maria dell'Anima and right into Piazza Navona.

Piazza Navona is sited over an ancient stadium, or circus, built by Emperor Domitian in approximately AD 80. The piazza retains the shape of this ancient

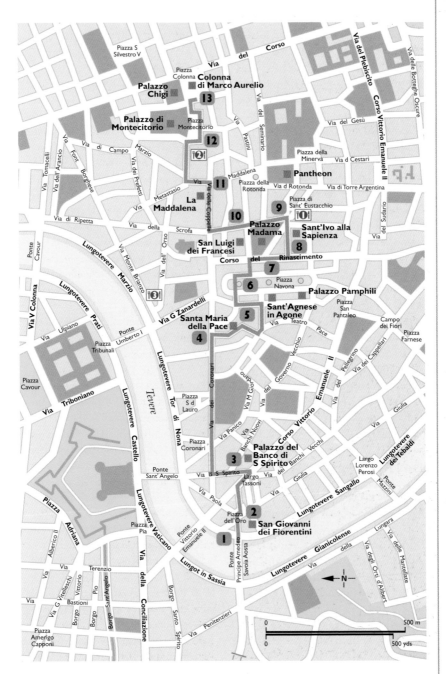

Piazza S
Silvestro V

Via del Corso

Via del Plebiscito

Via delle Botteghe Oscure

Piazza
Colonna

Colonna
di Marco Aurelio

Palazzo
Chigi

13

Corso Vittorio Emanuele II

Via del Seminario

Palazzo di
Montecitorio

Piazza
Montecitorio

12

Via del Gesù

Via di Campo

Via Fonti Borghese

Via della Arancio

Via dei Prefetti

Marzio

Via dei Pastini

Piazza della
Minerva

Via d Cestari

Via delle Coppelle

Maddalena

Piazza della
Rotonda

Pantheon

Via d Rotonda

Via di Torre Argentina

11

Metastasio

La
Maddalena

Via

della

Piazza della
Rotonda

Via di Ripetta

Via

della

Scrofa

10

9

Piazza di
Sant' Eustacchio

Palazzo
Madama

Sant'Ivo alla
Sapienza

Via

Via di Monte Brianzo

Via dell' Orso

San Luigi
dei Francesi

8

Corso del Rinascimento

Ponte
Cavour

Lungotevere Marzio

7

Via V Colonna

Lungotevere Prati

Via

Ulpiano

Ponte
Umberto I

Via G Zanardelli

6

Piazza
Navona

Palazzo Pamphili

Piazza
San
Pantaleo

Campo
dei Fiori

Via

Triboniano

Lungotevere Castello

Piazza
Tribunali

Santa Maria
della Pace

5

Sant'Agnese
in Agone

Via Teatro

Pace

Piazza
Farnese

Piazza
Cavour

Tevere

4

Lungotevere Tor di Nona

Piazza
S d
Lauro

Via dei Coronari

Via Vecchio

Via M Gio

Via del Governo

Via del Pellegrino

Via dei Cappellari

Giulia

Piazza
Coronari

Via Panico

Via Banchi Nuovi

Corso Vittorio Emanuele II

3

Palazzo del
Banco di
S Spirito

Via dei Banchi Vecchi

Largo
Lorenzo
Perosi

Lungotevere dei Tebaldi

Ponte
Sant'Angelo

Via B S Spirito

Largo
Tassoni

Via Giulia

Ponte
Mazzini

Piazza
Adriana

Ponte
Sant' Angelo

Ponte
Pia

Piazza
Pia

Ponte
Vittorio
Emanuele II

Piazza
dell'Oro

2

San Giovanni
dei Fiorentini

Lungotevere Sangallo

Lungara

Via degli Orti d'Alibert

Via delle Mantellate

Piazza
Adriana

Via
Alberico II

Via
Terenzio

Lungotevere Vaticano

1

Principe Amedeo

Savoia Aosta

Via Paola

Lungot in Sassia

Lungotevere Gianicolense

della

Via Alberico II

Via G
Vitelleschi

Vittorio

Pio

Bastioni

Borgo
Sant'Angelo

Borgo

Santo

Via Penitenzieri

Spirito

Via della Conciliazione

Piazza
Amerigo
Capponi

Borgo

←N→

0 _____ 500 m

0 _____ 500 yds

structure: you can trace it in the curved buildings that face the square on the north side. Bernini's Fountain of the Four Rivers stands at the centre and is beautifully illuminated in the evening. The wealthy Pamphili Pope Innocent X had the fountain, the church of Sant'Agnese facing the fountain and the adjacent Palazzo Pamphili renovated during his papacy (1644-55) because this was his family home. Borromini designed the façade of Sant'Agnese church, which is dedicated to one of the youngest martyrs of early Christianity. She was only 13 when she was beheaded. The antagonism between Bernini and Borromini is said to be expressed in the female statue on the right-hand summit of the church – she disdainfully averts her gaze from the fountain. Likewise, the figure representing the river Ganges in Bernini's fountain seems to hold up his hand in horror at the church façade. While the work greatly pleased his patron, Bernini himself was not so proud of the fountain. Passing in his carriage, he pulled down the blinds saying, "How ashamed I am to have done so poorly."

6 Leave Piazza Navona down Corsia Agonale to Corso Rinascimento.

Directly across Corso Rinascimento is the 16th-century Palazzo Madama, built by Giacomo della Porta for the powerful Medici family. Its name refers to Madam Margherita of Austria, wife of Alessandro de Medici. Today the mansion is the seat of the Italian Senate, and as such always heavily guarded.

7 Turn right down Corso del Rinascimento to No. 40.

Sant'Ivo alla Sapienza was originally the chapel at the heart of the old university of Rome until the latter was moved to modern premises in 1935. This beautiful gem of Baroque Rome is one of the testaments to Borromini's genius. It was designed in the shape of a bumblebee to symbolize the Barberini family of Pope Urban VIII, who originally commissioned the chapel. The ornate spire is inspired by the concept of the Tower of Babel. Inside, its stark white walls let you appreciate the clever architectural forms. An image of the holy dove surmounts the oval dome.

8 Turn right out of the church back up Corso Rinascimento. Turn right on Via degli Staderari.

The small wall fountain known as the Fountain of Books (1927) incorporates a stag's head, the symbol of the Sant'Eustachio district. The books are a reference to the nearby university.

9 Turn left on Via della Dogana Vecchia to Piazza San Luigi dei Francesi.

San Luigi dei Francesi, the French national church dedicated to that country's patron saint, was built during the course of the 16th century. Inside it holds Caravaggio's poignant three-work series depicting the life of St Matthew. Caravaggio was the consummate rebel artist of the Baroque. He was quarrelsome and frequently in trouble with the law

and the church. In 1606, after a bar room brawl that ended badly, he had to flee Rome on charges of manslaughter. He was pardoned by the pope, but died of malaria while on his homeward journey and was never reunited with the city. He was only 38 years old.

10 Continue up Via della Scrofa and turn right on Via delle Coppelle to Piazza della Maddalena.

The Maddalena church, dedicated to Mary Magdalene, is a rare example of Rococo architecture in Rome.

11 Turn left on Via della Maddalena. Turn right on Via della Uffici del Vicasio, continuing into Piazza Montecitorio.

Archaeologists tell us that in ancient times this was the site where emperors were cremated. Today the Palazzo Montecitorio houses the Lower House of Italian Parliament. Its first architect, Bernini, built it over the site of an old palace belonging to the Colonna family.

Before the palace stands an obelisk from Heliopolis that was erected here in 1792. In ancient Rome it stood at the centre of an enormous sundial on the Campus Martius or Field of Mars.

12 Continue through Piazza Montecitorio to the adjacent Piazza Colonna.

The centre of this square is dominated by the triumphal funerary column of Marcus Aurelius (AD 161-180). Like the column of Trajan it has an interior spiral staircase and its exterior relief sculptures depict the emperor's successful military campaigns. The Palazzo Chigi, on the the north side of the square, was built in 1592 for the wealthy Aldobrandini family of Pope Clement VIII. It was bought in 1659 by the Chigi Pope Alexander VII for his beloved nephews. Today it is the seat of the Presidente del Consiglio, the head of the Italian government.

13 The walk ends here. You can take buses 62, 63, 95 or 116 from Via del Corso.

DETAIL OF FOUNTAIN, PIAZZA NAVONA

The Road that Leads to Rome

Enter Rome from the north and walk down the ancient Via Flaminia in the footsteps of pagan merchants and tired pilgrims.

As the saying goes, 'All roads lead to Rome.' The ancient Via Flaminia, now known as Via del Corso, was a busy route bringing travellers into the city through the northern gate. During the Middle Ages, scores of pilgrims would arrive in Rome on foot or by mule, horse and/or carriage. You can still follow the ancient road into the heart of the current city centre before heading across the river to more modern areas. Today, Via del Corso is one of Rome's busiest shopping districts. It is also an interesting example of ancient Roman road-building that is today often obscured by later medieval and Renaissance rebuilding. The Via del Corso retains its very straight route through the centre of the city from Piazza del Popolo to Piazza Venezia. Walking this route you will experience the way Rome weaves together the various eras of its history into an ordered but colourful tapestry. You will visit Christian churches, imperial tombs, Renaissance piazzas and modern buildings.

1 Take Metro Line A to Flaminio and leave the station by the exit to Piazzale Flaminio.

From Piazzale Flaminio you can see the Porta del Popolo, which served as the northern gateway into Rome. The 16th-century design by Nanni di Baccio Bigio, who name is worth a laugh, is modelled on a triumphal arch and decorated with ancient columns and statues.

2 Pass under Porta del Popolo.

You can now see the side of the gateway designed for Pope Alexander VII by Bernini to welcome one of Rome's most illustrious and wealthy pilgrims, Queen Christina of Sweden. The pope greeted her warmly on first arrival, but over time he would lose his patience with this eccentric visitor. To the left stands Santa Maria del Popolo. This church was built over the site of Nero's tomb. A tree once marked this spot and, according to legend, it was possessed by the cursed spirit of the former emperor. Pope Paschal II had the tree felled and its ashes thrown into the river. He then built a chapel to the Virgin Mary over the site. A larger construction was built in 1227 and expanded during the Renaissance. Martin Luther stayed here on his visit to Rome in 1512, when he was disgusted by Catholic corruption and vice. This church is a treasure trove of art. The Chigi chapel inside was designed by Raphael. Caravaggio's *Conversion of St Paul* (1601) and *Crucifixion of St*

Peter (1600-1601) are within the Cerasi chapel. The realism of Caravaggio's divine characters often got him in trouble with the church, which preferred to imagine Mary and Jesus as icons of ideal beauty.

3 Cross Piazza del Popolo.

This piazza was first designed in the 16th century. Its obelisk was erected in 1589 under Pope Sixtus V, who seems to have had particular fetish for obelisks – he had them erected throughout the city. Giuseppe Valadier completed the piazza by adding the surrounding walls and statuary in 1816-20. Santa Maria dei Miracoli and Santa Maria in Montesanto are the so-called 'twin' churches that mark the entrance to Via del Corso.

DISTANCE 1 mile (1.6km)

ALLOW 1.5 hours

START Flaminio Piazza del Popolo Metro

FINISH Piazza Cavour

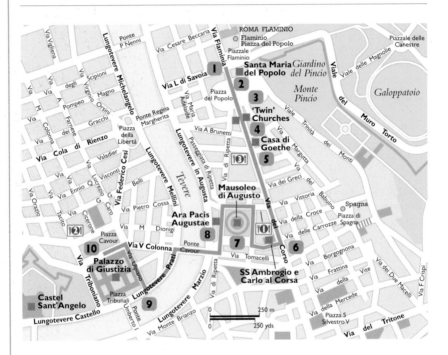

Actually they are not identical. See if you can spot the differences.

4 Continue straight down Via del Corso to Goethe's house at No. 18.

This was once ancient Via Flaminia, built in 220 BC as a principal route to the Adriatic. During the Renaissance it was renamed Via del Corso after the races, or *corse*, that took place along the thoroughfare as part of the carnival. Today it is the city's busiest shopping street.

The house of German author Johann Wolfgang von Goethe, who lived here from 1786–88, is right at the centre of the city. He later wrote that he was never again as happy as he had been in Rome. **GOETHE'S HOUSE;** OPEN TUE–SUN 10–6; www.casadigoethe.it

5 Continue down Via del Corso to Largo San Carlo al Corso.

On the right is the church of St Ambrose and St Carlo. It was donated to the

OPPOSITE: OBELISK OF PHARAOH RAMESES II

Lombard community by Pope Sixtus IV in 1471. The Lombards, northern Italians of today, dedicated it to St Ambrose, patron saint of Milan and early church leader and reformer. Charles Borromeo, founder of the Trinitarian order, was canonized in 1610 and the church was re-dedicated to both saints.

6 Turn right after the church on Vicolo del Grottino to Piazza Imperatore Augusto.

Here you see the remains of the mausoleum built for Emperor Augustus and his family. When this sepulchre was constructed in 26 BC it was the most glorious of its kind, modelled on the mausoleum of Alexander the Great in Alexandria. Today only its brick substructure and the cypress trees remain as an ode to the first emperor's resting place. Two obelisks once marked its entrance and these now stand on the Esquiline and Quirinal Hills. The structure became a Colonna family fortress in the Middle Ages and was later used as gardens and a concert venue.

7 Turn right, moving anticlockwise around the mausoleum and left on Via Ara Pacis. The entrance to the Ara Pacis faces south off Via di Ripetta.

Ara Pacis, the Altar of Peace, celebrates the Pax Romana and the Golden Age of

ARA PACIS

Augustus. The rule of Augustus between 27 BC and AD 14 was a peaceful time in which Rome flourished culturally. Augustus was a patron of the arts and avidly sought to make Rome a beautiful capital city that would rival Athens or Alexandria. Augustus was a good leader, but his rise to power meant the end of the ancient democratic Roman Republic. The altar is a monument of propaganda, praising the new dictator as a Roman hero. Beautiful relief sculptures depict mythological and allegorical subjects. The exterior lateral walls show members of the imperial family engaged in a solemn religious procession.

ARA PACIS; OPEN TUE-SUN 9-7

8 Leave the Ara Pacis complex heading south to Lungotevere Marzio and cross left across Ponte Cavour. Turn left along Lungotevere Prati.

WHERE TO EAT

🍽️ **IL VERO ALFREDO,**
Piazza Augusto Imperatore 30;
Tel: 06 6878734.
This restaurant has an international reputation and is known for its *fettucine al burro.*

🍽️ **ENOTECA COSTANTINI,**
Piazza Cavour 16;
Tel: 06 3203575.
This wine bar's elaborately decorated exterior has a grapevine design.

🍽️ **AL VANTAGGIO,**
Via del Vantaggio 35;
Tel: 06 3236848.
Roman and Calabrian cuisine served in a relaxed atmosphere – you can sit inside or out.

The river brought travellers into and out of the city in more than one sense. During Roman times the Tiber was navigable and barges brought goods from throughout the empire. In the Dark Ages, countless numbers of murdered citizens and visitors had to be fished from the river. The massive edifice of the Palazzo della Giustizia, Justice Palace, was finished in 1911 after 22 years of delays and a bill of around 40 million lire. Despite all the trouble taken to build this modern eyesore, it is derisively known as the *Palazzaccio*, the decrepit or rotten palace. Its heavy travertine blocks are sinking into the soft earth that naturally flanks the river, and engineers are still trying to save it. It is decorated with statues of famous Italian jurists.

9 Turn right along Via Ulpiano around the Palazzaccio to Piazza Cavour.

This piazza is a perfect rectangle. It is named after Count Camillo Benso Cavour, chief minister to the King of Sardinia and major political figure of Italian Unification. His commemorative statue, sculpted by Stefano Galletti in 1895, stands on a raised plinth in the centre of the piazza.

10 The walk ends here. Take bus 30, 280, or 492 from Piazza Cavour.

Fascist Places and Spaces

An excursion that ventures outside central Rome to explore the fascist architecture and museums of the suburban EUR district.

EUR, designed on a modern urban plan, is a district three miles south of Rome. The letters stand for Esposizione Universale Romana (World Roman Expo) – the area was originally built for a World Fair intended to celebrate the 20th anniversary of the fascist march on Rome in 1922, when fascists took control of government. This so-called 'march' was glorified by the regime as a victory, but in reality it was not very militaristic in nature. Instead of temporary exhibition halls, Mussolini wanted to build a grand urban area in the imperial style. He hired architect Marcello Piacentini, the predominant architect under fascism, to begin its construction in 1938. Fascist art and architecture uses monumental size and austere classical forms both to aggrandize the authoritarian regime and to celebrate Rome's illustrious imperial past. Italy's entrance into World War II prevented the Expo from taking place. Construction was interrupted and most of the buildings were not finished until the 1950s. Nowadays, the district is marked by its greenery and wide straight streets.

1 Take Metro Line B to EUR Palasport. You will come out onto Viale America. Head north on Viale America and turn right on Viale Beethoven, then turn left on Viale Europa. At the end of Viale Europa, cross the intersection and climb the stairs to SS Pietro e Paolo.

This modern church was built on the highest point in EUR and dedicated to St Peter and St Paul. Its hemispherical dome has a diameter of 105ft (32m). Viale Europa is known for its lovely shops.

2 Leave the church and head back down Viale Europa before turning left on Viale Pasteur and following the road to the end.

At the end of Viale Pasteur you cannot miss the Palazzo della Civiltà, designed by Giovanni Guerrini, Ernesto Bruno La Padula and Mario Romano. Commonly known as the 'square coliseum', this building has been featured in movies like *Hudson Hawk* (1991) and *Titus Andronicus* (1999). The inscription displayed on all four sides is a bold ode to the Italian people. It reads: 'A people of poets, of artists, of heroes, of saints, of thinkers, of scientists, of navigators, of voyagers.'

3 Head right down Viale della Civiltà del Lavoro. Turn left on Viale dell' Agricoltura.

The Piazzale dell'Agricoltura and Piazzale dell'Industria − piazzas of Agriculture and Industry − celebrate the fascist concept of national economic

WHERE TO EAT

🍴 **MACINANTI LA PIZZERIA,**
Via Elio Vittorini 45;
Tel: 06 5010222. www.macinanti.it
A family-run pizzeria with a wood oven and offering a wide selection of meat and fish.

🍴 **CAFFE PALOMBINI,**
Piazzale Konrad Adenauer 12;
Tel: 06 5911700.
A Roman pasticceria serving ice cream, cakes and coffee.

planning and regulation. Fabulous fountains and greenery delineate the elongated rectangle.

4 Turn right down Via Cristoforo Colombo.

In the original plan for EUR, called E42, the Piazza delle Nazioni Unite was to be a grand entrance gate called Porta Imperiale. The road now known as Via Cristoforo Colombo was to be called the Via Imperiale. Of course, these names were chosen to allude to Rome's glorious imperial past and suggest a new beginning under fascism. Adjustments had to be made after the collapse of the regime. The concave buildings now house the National Insurance offices. Via Cristoforo Columbo is the main route to the beach of Ostia.

5 Continue down Via Cristoforo Colombo to Piazza G Marconi.

OPPOSITE: PALAZZO DELLA CIVILTÀ

DISTANCE **1 mile (1.6km)**

ALLOW **2 hours**

START **EUR Palasport Metro**

FINISH **EUR Fermi Metro or EUR Palasport Metro**

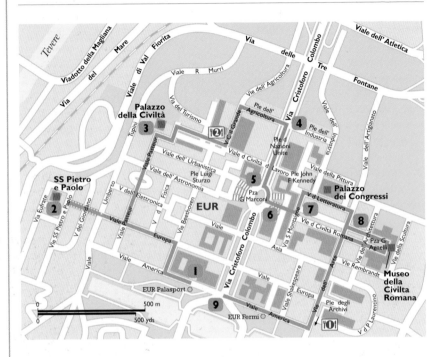

At the centre of the busy traffic roundabout stands a monument to Guglielmo Marconi (1874–1937), the Italian physicist and inventor of wireless communication. His discoveries led to the development of radio, telephone and television. The modern 148ft (45m) high obelisk was designed by Arturo Dazzi (1881–1966) and depicts Marconi's considerable achievements. The buildings on the left house museums of science, prehistory and the National Museum of the High Middle Ages.

6 Turn left from Piazza Marconi on Viale della Civiltà Romana. Turn left on Via Montaigne to reach Piazza John Kennedy.

The Palazzo dei Congressi dominates the piazza. Its novel dome was finished in 1954 by architect Adalberto Libera. Inside the meeting hall, Salone dei Ricevimenti, is a 125ft (38m) cube large enough to hold the entire Pantheon, and decorated with mosaics and frescos by Italian modernists like Achille Funi and Gino

Severini. During the summer its rooftop terrace becomes a lively open-air disco.

7 Turn right down Viale della Letteratura, right down Viale dell'Arte and left down Viale della Civiltà Romana to reach the Museum of Roman Civilization.

The museum is filled with miniatures and plaster-cast reproductions of art. **MUSEUM OF ROMAN CIVILIZATION;** OPEN TUE-SAT 9-2, SUN 9-1.30; www.museociviltaromana.it

8 Turn back down Viale della Civiltà Romana and turn left on Viale dell'Arte. Turn right on Viale America.

Enter the Parco Centrale del Lago on your left. You can walk around this man-made lake if you like. An axial view from the foot of Via Cristoforo Colombo leads the eye over the lake, up the so-called Garden of the Falls, and frames the dome of the Palazzo dello Sport, also known as the Palalottomatica. Rome's major sports complex, it was designed by Pier Luigi Nervi and Marcello Piacentini for the 1960 Summer Olympics. Its dome is 312ft (95m) across and it can hold 11,200 seated spectators. Concerts and sporting events are held here regularly.

9 The walk ends here. The entrance to Metro Line B stations EUR Fermi and EUR Palasport are on Viale America.

INDEX

ACKNOWLEDGEMENTS

The Automobile Association wishes to thank the following photographers and organisations for their assistance in the preparation of this book. Abbreviations for the picture credits are as follows – (b/g) background; (AA) AA World Travel Library

Front Cover: Tiber river with Ponte S Angelo and Dome of St Peters, Ernst Wrba/Alamy

3 AA/S McBride; 6-7 b/g AA; 8 AA/J Holmes; 11 AA/S McBride; 12 AA/S McBride; 14 Ian M Butterfield/Alamy; 17 Andrea Matone/Alamy; 18 AA/S McBride; 20-21 Randy Wells/Getty Images; 22 JLImages/Alamy; 25 Jon Arnold Images/Alamy; 27 AA/P Wilson; 28 Mark O'Flaherty/Alamy; 29 AA/C Sawyer; 31 Pictures Colour Library; 32-33 AA/J Holmes; 34-35 AA/J Holmes; 36 AA/J Holmes; 39 AA/S McBride; 40 Andrea Matone/Alamy; 41 AA/S McBride; 42 CuboImages/Robert Harding; 43 AA/A Kouprianoff; 45 AA/S McBride; 47 AA/J Holmes; 48-49 AA/J Holmes; 50 Pictures Colour Library; 51 John Heseltine; 53 AA/J Holmes; 54 AA/D Miterdiri; 56 AA/J Holmes; 57 AA/J Holmes; 59 Adam Eastland/Alamy; 60 AA/J Holmes; 62-63 David Angel/Alamy; 64 AA/D Miterdiri; 65 AA/J Holmes; 67 AA/S McBride; 69 John Heseltine; 70 AA/S McBride; 73 Michael Juno/Alamy; 74 AA/S McBride; 75 James Osmond/Alamy; 76-77 Pictures Colour Library; 78 AA/C Sawyer; 81 AA/J Holmes; 83 AA/D Miterdiri; 84 Robert Stainforth/Alamy; 87 Iconotec/Alamy; 88 John Heseltine; 90-91 AA/D Miterdiri; 92 AA/C Sawyer; 93 AA/J Holmes; 95 AA/C Sawyer; 97 AA/C Sawyer; 98 CuboImages srl/Alamy; 99 Giovanni Guarino/Alamy; 101 Glyn Thomas/Alamy; 102 AA/D Miterdiri; 104-105 Eddie Gerald/Alamy; 106 Michael Hunt; 107 AA/J Holmes; 109 Michael Hunt; 111 Michael Hunt; 112 AA/D Miterdiri; 113 AA/J Holmes; 115 AA/D Miterdiri; 116-117 AA/D Miterdiri; 118-119 CuboImages srl/Alamy; 120 AA/C Sawyer; 121 Pictures Colour Library; 123 AA/P Wilson; 124 Peter Horree/Alamy; 126 AA/J Holmes; 127 AA/J Holmes; 129 John Heseltine; 131 AA/J Holmes; 132-133 imagebroker/Alamy; 134 AA/S McBride; 137 AA/S McBride; 139 AA/S McBride; 140 AA; 141 Pictures Colour Library; 143 The Travel Library/Stuart Black; 144 John Heseltine; 146-147 AA/S McBride; 148 Mark Bassett/Alamy; 151 Rough Guides/Alamy; 152-153 John Heseltine; 154 AA/J Holmes; 156 AA/P Wilson; 159 AA/S McBride; 160-161 AA/S McBride; 162 Rough Guides/Alamy; 163 AA/J Holmes; 165 AA/J Holmes; 166 AA/D Miterdiri; 168 AA/C Sawyer; 171 AA/C Sawyer; 172-173 Oliviero Olivieri/Robert Harding.

Every effort has been made to trace the copyright holders, and we apologise in advance for any unintentional omissions or errors. We would be pleased to apply any corrections in any following edition of this publication.